D1024853

EDITING TWENTIETH-CENTURY TEXTS

OTHER VOLUMES IN THIS SERIES

Editing Sixteenth-Century Texts edited by R.J. Schoeck

Editing Nineteenth-Century Texts edited by John M. Robson

Editing Eighteenth-Century Texts edited by D.I.B. Smith

Editor, Author, and Publisher edited by Wm. J. Howard

Editing Twentieth Century Texts

Papers given at the
Editorial Conference
University of Toronto, November 1969

EDITED BY FRANCESS G. HALPENNY

Published for the Editorial Conference Committee
University of Toronto
by University of Toronto Press

Toronto and Buffalo
Printed in Canada

ISBN 0-8020-3276-1
Microfiche ISBN 0-8020-0020-7
LC 72-151371

Contents

Contributors vii

Introduction 3
FRANCESS G. HALPENNY

A Proposal for a CEAA Edition of William Faulkner 12
JAMES B. MERIWETHER

'A Might Collation': Animadversions on the Text of F. Scott Fitzgerald 28
MATTHEW J. BRUCCOLI

Editing Hofmannsthal: Some Remarks Concerning a New Edition 51
RICHARD EXNER

Editing a Manuscript: Virginia Woolf's *The Waves* 77
JOHN W. GRAHAM

A Note on Editing *The Interpreters*, A Novel by Wole Soyinka 93
ELDRED D. JONES

Members of the Conference 102

Contributors

MATTHEW J. BRUCCOLI, professor of English at the University of South Carolina and director of the Center of Editions of American Authors, is the author of *The Composition of Tender is the Night* (1963) and editor of *The Fitzgerald/Hemingway Annual* (1969-). His other publications include *Ernest Hemingway, Cub Reporter* (1970); *As Ever Scott Fitz: The F. Scott Fitzgerald/Harold Ober Correspondence* (1971), *F. Scott Fitzgerald in His Own Time* (1971), *Kenneth Millar/Ross Macdonald: A Checklist* (1971), and *Ernest Hemingway's Oak Park Apprenticeship* (1971). He is general editor of the Pittsburgh Series in Bibliography.

RICHARD EXNER, professor of German at the University of California at Santa Barbara, has been working for several years on Hugo von Hofmannsthal. His *Index Nominum* of Hofmannsthal's works will soon be published by Lothar Stiehm Verlag, Heidelberg. He is currently preparing a collection and evaluation of Hofmannsthal's conversations.

J.W. GRAHAM is a professor of English at the University of

Western Ontario. Aside from his edition of the manuscript of *The Waves*, he is currently at work on a critical study of Virginia Woolf. His major interests are modern poetry, modern fiction, and the study of long narratives.

ELDRED D. JONES, professor of English at Fourah Bay College, University of Sierra Leone, was educated at Fourah Bay College and Corpus Christi College, Oxford. He is author of *Othello's Countrymen* (Oxford) and *The Elizabethan Image of Africa* (University of Virginia) and edits *African Literature Today*. He is also co-editor of *Adjustments: An Anthology of African and Western Prose* (Edward Arnold), and *Freetown: A Symposium* (Sierra Leone University Press). He is at present working on a critical study of Wole Soyinka.

JAMES B. MERIWETHER is a McClintock Professor of Southern Letters at the University of South Carolina. He is the author of *The Literary Career of William Faulkner* (1961), textual editor of the Centennial Edition of William Gilmore Simms, and a member of the Executive Committee of the Center for Editions of American Authors.

EDITING TWENTIETH-CENTURY TEXTS

Introduction

FRANCESS G. HALPENNY

The annual Toronto conference on problems and opportunities in the editing of texts turned in 1969 to the twentieth century, in response both to suggestions from its own continuing members and to the fact that editorial activities for authors of this century are particularly lively at present. In part those activities have links with the undertakings of the CEAA, the Center for Editions of American Authors, whose parent organization is the Modern Language Association. The preparation of definitive texts by those connected with its editions of American classics has attracted much attention and led to a vigorous discussion, in articles and books, of principles and methods. The conference was pleased to have had as one of its speakers Matthew J. Bruccoli, the director of the Center. At the end of the year following the conference it became possible for the kind of textual apparatus described by another of our speakers, James B. Meriwether, in connection with William Faulkner, to receive the formal seal of approval of the Cen-

Members of the Committee for the 1969 conference were: J.D. Baird, G.E. Bentley, Jr, David Esplin, Francess G. Halpenny, Wm J. Howard, J.A. McClelland, R.J. Schoeck, and D.I.B. Smith.

ter, and the conference has particular pleasure in recording this recent decision.

Faulkner, Fitzgerald, Hofmannsthal, Virginia Woolf are undeniably, in the 1970s, classic authors of the twentieth century and there would seem to be no incongruity in a concern for reliable texts or in a study of their methods of writing by examining various kinds of documents associated with the texts of their works as published. Professor Graham's efforts to provide careful, clear, readable, cross-referenced versions of Mrs Woolf's early drafts of *The Waves* are an example of the second activity. In the edition outlined in his paper he has much in mind the access of a group of readers larger than the limited number who would be prepared or able to work with a facsimile alone. To their group he offers, in full, the means of studying for themselves the early composition of a major work. Yet he does not have to rely on elaborately contrived and expensive typographical devices to give a printed representation of the pages of the notebooks; he is using the flexibility and economy of a modern sophisticated typewriter and offset lithography to reproduce exactly even interlineations, strike-outs, and marginalia. Undoubtedly this kind of presentation and reproduction will be increasingly accepted and increasingly used. At the conference Professor Jack Dalton spoke of the challenges in working with versions of *Finnegans Wake* (unfortunately it was not possible to include his paper in this volume), and the methods just mentioned would seem to have their value also in the editorial handling of such complicated manuscript material as Joyce offers.

The conference was pleased to hear of the discussion surrounding the immense labours of the definitive edition of Hofmannsthal now going forward in Europe, with editorial contributions from North America. Professor Exner prepared his paper for the conference when this courageous edition was in the early stages of exploration of scope and method; he sets forth vividly the volume and complexity of the materials to be examined and the intricacies of organization required simply to bring together, let alone harmonize, the work of many contributors. The planning for the edition has of course continued since his paper was given and its direction has become more certain. (His note on page 63 indicates consecutive developments over the succeeding months.) The account is historically interesting and valuable as showing what has to be reckoned with in this kind of editorial undertaking. Collaborative effort on a large editorial project is a present-day phenomenon, especially in North America, aided technically by, inter alia, microfilm and tape recorders, air communication for editors and their correspondence, and the manifold distributions of the copying machine, but more essentially encouraged by the skills of a growing body of textual editors, by the emergence of institutions with the funds to sponsor or assist the research involved, and by the ability, largely of university presses, to publish them. The edition of Hofmannsthal offers for a twentieth-century author the kind of service being rendered for authors of other centuries: two of these editions, for John Stuart Mill and Erasmus (in English), have their editorial centre on the home ground of the conference. As Professor Exner's paper demonstrates, there are always large questions of size and completeness for the edition as a whole, of the structure to be given to texts and apparatus, of the arrangement to be assigned to works in the volumes of the edition, of how editors are to decide what is essential context for the texts they prepare and what use is to be made of the manuscript materials, with their variants, from which the final printed works emerged. What has to be defined, eventually, for such a multi-volume project, is, as Professor Exner underlines, a 'possible' edition: one which will not soon be superseded but which will not take an unacceptable number of years to prepare.

The holdings of the Berg Collection in New York include the manuscript materials worked upon by Professor Graham in Ontario by means of film copies. In the future such collections, especially for the later twentieth century, will be sizeable as a result of the current acquisitiveness of librarians and their assisting scholars; this eagerness has already encouraged living authors not to throw away, and sales of their working papers, from first-draft manuscript jottings to printer's proofs, are recorded regularly. The problems of textual editing may well be made easier by so much evidence, but they could also become more complex. Think, for instance, of the difficulty in working out the timing and reliability of many authorial or stenographic retypings of passages to produce more legible copy or to incorporate revisions drafted on rough pages later destroyed. There might also be the necessity of determining the authority to be given to undated Xerox copies of a typescript, made at different times for different purposes and therefore with differing amounts of alteration or correction. There is also likely to be in future the problem of authors who 'write' initially in whole or in part by using a tape recorder, the transcripts from which are corrected effectively by themselves into copy, or perhaps gone over too quickly; if tapes are reused after erasures, where is certainty to be found?

But to dwell on these possibilities is to turn away from texts requiring attention now. As Professor Bruccoli points out forcefully, a respect for good texts of modern authors has too rarely been seen by literary critics and scholars to be a 'basic need,' in Professor Meriwether's phrase, although this apathy seems to be decreasing now. The explanation for the apathy may be found partly, one suspects, in an obliviousness to the need for constant watchfulness in the reproduction of words by typing or printing or in a lazy impatience with the necessity of textual fidelity. (To take examples somewhat by the way, requests sent by authors or editors to publishers for permission to quote passages from their books are usually found to contain errors in the citation of the relevant lines, and editors of anthologies frequently submit as copy Xerox versions of their chosen excerpts which they have not examined even for typographical errors.) But, as the essays in this volume point out, the lack of attention given to reliable twentieth-century texts may also be explained by two unavoidable facts: authors achieve only with time the status that makes their every work a subject for close scrutiny, and they have also usually received, and indeed should receive, much other study before the quality of their texts becomes a crucial and a possible concern; the copyright held by commercial publishers, who may not always be willing or able to see to correction of the texts they keep in print, can discourage editors and make it necessary for those who persist to develop editorial devices which will at once respect copyright and provide the means for emendation. The papers on Faulkner and Fitzgerald present practical suggestions for dealing with copyrighted texts in accordance with modern scholarly methods.

Editors of the texts of earlier centuries have been accustomed to pay much attention to the practices of printers in producing books, and have even been able on some occasions to determine how a shift from one compositor to another could affect the presentation in print. Indeed, as R.C. Bald has noted, 'most of the conventions of English spelling and punctuation are the creation of printers and compositors, especially in the seventeenth century.'[1] The editor preparing a twentieth-century text requires, it should almost go without saying, a full acquaintance with the methods of modern printers, and also of modern publishers, as is implied in the papers on Faulkner and Fitzgerald. These printing and publishing procedures are seldom those of the small, personal shop of earlier centuries, and they certainly have a bearing on modern texts. A modern manuscript, as noted above, is likely to reach a publisher after a varying amount of typing, retyping, and copying has occurred while it was in the author's or agent's hand. The publisher's decision to publish will be based not on the exactness of each *t* and *i* on the pages he reads but rather on the effect of the words as a literary structure. He

1 / R.C. Bald, 'Editorial Problems - A Preliminary Survey,' *Studies in Bibliography* 3 (1951) 6

may suggest to the author that revision would be desirable or necessary to make publication possible by his firm, and revision, and therefore physical reworking, of the manuscript may occur before it leaves the author's keeping. The manuscript as accepted for publication will thus have been put through a typewriter in whole or in part several times by the author himself or his typist(s), and it will differ from the author's first draft by changes or corrections he himself made along the way (therefore authoritative) or by accidents of transcription that he has not noticed. Authors are often not observant of such accidents and indeed can take a careless attitude to them.

The typescript will now usually be given to an editor in the publishing house for preparation for printing. The detection of typographical and other inadvertent errors, the noting of what seem puzzling details in phrasing or fact, and an attention to accidentals of punctuation and capitalization in the interests of a reasonable consistency are a normal part of any such editor's duty. Beyond this duty lie other possibilities of inquiry related to words and meanings and structure, depending on the amount of scrutiny a manuscript is thought to need, depending also on the time and money that can be devoted to the editorial reading as a whole. The kind of work being published must, of course, have an important bearing on what a publisher's editor does - the individualistic, idiosyncratic expression of a modern poet and often of a modern novelist require an approach different from that for expository prose. The actual results of this editorial reading will be determined inevitably by the skill and experience and sensitivity of the editor. They will be determined also by the amount of consultation with the author, and the care he takes to consider, and approve or not approve, what is marked, suggested, or queried.

The conference found itself in lively discussion of this particular aspect of modern publishing, and hence the attention given to it in this introduction. (I should confess here that since I have myself passed many years as an editor, in a university press, my personal interest must be allowed for.) Some editors of texts in creative literature have tended to view publisher's editors as intruders whose work, being largely an unwarranted interference, should rarely be given any authority. It is quite true that the editorial work may be ineptly or too hastily done (the latter can certainly happen when the schedule of production is tight or the budget does not allow for much more than a quick overview); as a result confusion or inaccuracy could be introduced. Moreover, the author may not have sufficient and effective chance to see the outcome of the editorial reading at some stage. Professor Meriwether aptly cites an unfortunate example, from a chapter of Faulkner, of how insensitive copy-editing attempted to improve the colloquial language of a Mississippi boy. One must wince at this, and wish that the editor had had an eye more alert to catch and solve the typographical puzzles that lurked in 'straw cow' and 'rese,bled' - puzzles like these could have been the subject of an acceptable marginal query to the author. It is also perhaps possible to speculate on what clarification of the confused time scheme of *Tender is the Night* might have occurred if some person had anticipated Professor Bruccoli's students who are troubled because 'after 1925 they can't tell what year they are in or how much time has elapsed since the opening of the novel.' In fairness, however, against 'misses,' must be offset gains. One cannot overlook the fact that it is a rare manuscript indeed today (as in the past) that reaches the publisher (or did reach the printer) with every word exactly in the place or the form the author might intend, with every phrase in the degree of clarity he might wish, with all its accidentals in a pattern decided upon by himself. The house editor enters upon a collaboration with the author in the interests of readers, and trustworthy collaboration should produce a text from which undesirable inadvertencies have been removed as far as possible and which the author approves as representing what he wants to say and how it is to be said.

The hazards for a text in the process of typesetting and proofreading are still common as in the past and they unfortunately do not decline. Standards of proofreading have been affected by rising costs of production, among other factors, and readers, perhaps conditioned somewhat by the lapses visible in newspapers, perforce grow more resigned. Following a modern text fully through its proof stages will require observation of all that might have happened (bearing in mind the special peculiarities of setting and changing in monotype, linotype, or on tape): the questions asked or changes made by the printer's and/or publisher's readers, the surveillance of proofs by the publisher's editor (who may not actually read proofs but only scrutinize them), the amount and kind of attention given by the author. The latter's proofs are important to the textual editor, for the changes he made or did not make. (Their importance is reflected in the correspondence that developed in the *TLS* in late 1970 over the ownership of author's proofs.) But the author's proofs are not usually the 'master' proofs - 'master' sets of galleys and pages and revised pages will likely be kept in the publisher's offices, and it is upon these that the corrections actually to be made by the printer will be entered. Thus the changes marked by the author might be altered or denied to avoid too much resetting (with his knowledge or perhaps not) or might be transcribed with some error. The author will usually not follow proofs through to revised pages. Since publishers have little room to store sets of proofs, most of this evidence may disappear once a book is printed. Thus, although there are today more complicated and elaborate machines to facilitate the preparation and presentation of literary works, and many eyes, from the author's on down the line, to view the successive processes, fidelity of representation in a first printing is far from assured, and careful review of twentieth-century texts which are shown to be of lasting value will be required. The description just given points to some of the problems of that review. The necessities of it are set forth in leading examples by Professor Meriwether and Professor Bruccoli in their papers.

They discuss the special problems of emendations in re-printings, which have often been fewer than accuracy would demand, sometimes inexplicably, sometimes because of the ominous effect that the cost of making corrections can have on the possibility of doing new editions. Both authors have investigated the possibility of 'do-it-yourself' kits, which could vary in scope and complexity, but which would always present the variations in available editions from an accepted text; the interested reader would simply use the kit to mark up his own copy of one of those editions. Professor Bruccoli has kindly allowed us to print three of these kits in this volume. It is our hope that students of Fitzgerald will find them helpful, and that they may serve as examples of editorial ingenuity applicable to other authors in need. The use of typescript to provide such 'kits' is referred to by Professor Meriwether, and this book itself is an example of it.

Our volume concludes with a guest essay by Professor Eldred D. Jones, which reflects yet another contemporary challenge: editorial commentary for English texts in the literature of countries where English is not necessarily the chief language of many of its readers. If this literature is to be appreciated more fully, these readers require assistance, but the amount and the kind are a special problem of tact. We are grateful to Professor Jones for giving us this introduction to an unusual contemporary editorial need.

The conference turned its attention in November 1970 to the editing of seventeenth-century texts, and in November 1971 will examine textual problems presented by the Romantics. Its members are grateful to the Canada Council and to the University of Toronto for their support of its meetings, which have now produced a series of five volumes.

A Proposal for a CEAA Edition of William Faulkner

JAMES B. MERIWETHER

In discussing here the past, the present, and, to a certain extent, I trust, the future of the text of William Faulkner, I begin with two assumptions: first, that a complete or substantially complete collected edition, intelligently planned, and with a reliable text, is the first requirement of the Faulkner field; and, second, that we have not got that edition now, nor are we likely to get it in the near future, unless extraordinary steps are taken, or unless some extraordinary stroke of good fortune intervenes.

Both assumptions, it seems to me, are axiomatic, granted the fact that Faulkner is an important twentieth-century American novelist; but it may be well to comment upon them briefly before proceeding.

So far as the first is concerned, literary critics and scholars can hardly afford to debate the proposition that an accurate (and available) text is their basic need, but we must remember that the making of such a text is generally the last task to be undertaken in the study of American novelists. Even the recognition of the need for such a text does not generally appear until late; indeed, this recognition has marked the coming of age, in a very real sense, of the critical and scholarly study of the major American novelists.

For it is obvious that a great deal of work must be done, by scholars and critics engaged in a wide variety of bibliographical, biographical, historical, and critical research, before we are likely to become aware of the inadequacies of the usual commercially produced texts that are the starting-point of our studies of the novel. Ultimately, we can expect, the critical and popular reputation of an important novelist will be sufficient to enable a publisher to undertake a collected edition. By then, we can hope, the study of that novelist will be sufficiently mature for there to be a general agreement upon the need for a well-edited text, and for there to be editors interested in the project and competent to carry it out. But we are more likely to find a novelist's reputation growing faster than the demand for a better text of his writings; and the limiting factors of copyright control and the lack of interested, capable editors may preclude the undertaking of a well-edited collected edition even when it is economically feasible. This is particularly true for our authors of the twentieth century, of course, most of whose works are controlled by their original commercial publishers; and today students of Faulkner and Hemingway are learning the lesson taught for so long in the Hawthorne and Melville fields: the necessity of living with inferior texts of superior novelists.

The validity of my second assumption - that we do not have a satisfactory text of Faulkner at the present time - has been obvious for some years now.[1] Many of his books were ineptly copy-edited; some were rigidly house-styled;

1 / I have called attention to various aspects of the problem in the following essays and papers: 'Some Notes on the Text of Faulkner's *Sanctuary,*' *Papers of the Bibliographical Society of America* 55 (1961) 192-206; 'Bibliographical and Textual Studies of Twentieth-Century Writers,' *Approaches to the Study of Twentieth-Century Literature* (East Lansing, Mich., 1962), 33-51 (Proceedings of the Conference in the Study of Twentieth-Century Literature, May 1961); 'Notes on the Textual History of *The Sound and the Fury,*' *Papers of the Bibliographical Society of America* 56 (1962) 285-316; 'The New Editions of William Faulkner,' a paper read before the Modern Language Association, New York, 28 December, 1964; and 'William Faulkner,' in *Fifteen Modern American Authors: A Survey of Research and Criticism,* ed. Jackson R. Bryer (Durham, NC, 1969) 175-210 (esp. 178-80).

some were bowdlerized; and one novel, *Sartoris*, was severely mauled in the process of being cut down by an editor to what was deemed an acceptable length. For much of his career Faulkner had little power to insist that his publishers carry out his intentions, and for most of it he seems to have been at best an indifferent proofreader of his own work.

Clearly, then, we need an edition of Faulkner more worthy of his literary importance. And such an edition is possible, for the major documents upon which it must be based, Faulkner's own manuscripts and typescripts, have in most cases survived, though there are some important gaps.[2] But we are unlikely to have this edition in the near future, for the texts of all Faulkner's novels are in copyright, and accordingly are controlled by a commercial publisher.[3] The same factors, therefore, that have prevented us from having satisfactory editions of the other major American novelists of the twentieth century are also responsible for our not having a better Faulkner text.

Basically, there are three factors involved in the control of an author's text by a commercial publisher which, so far, have precluded the undertaking of the editions we so badly need of Faulkner and Fitzgerald, of Hemingway and Wolfe. The first of these concerns the planning of such an edition. The manifold responsibilities of an editor for a commercial publisher are not likely to leave him time to acquire the knowledge and experience which would enable him to plan a comprehensive edition of a major novelist.

2 / Apparently there did not survive either typescript printer's copy or any proofs of the first four novels (*Soldiers' Pay, Mosquitoes, Sartoris,* and *The Sound and the Fury*), though Faulkner kept, among his own papers, complete typescript or carbon typescript versions of all four, and complete manuscript versions of the last two. The lack of printer's copy or proofs of *Sartoris* and *The Sound and the Fury* is particularly troublesome. Faulkner deposited his papers in the Princeton University Library in 1957, and transferred them to the University of Virginia Library in 1959. They are listed and briefly described in James B. Meriwether, *The Literary Career of William Faulkner* (Princeton 1961).

3 / *Soldiers' Pay* and *Mosquitoes* are published by Liveright; Faulkner's other books are controlled by Random House.

Even in the improbable event that someone else had already accomplished the indispensable basic bibliographical research, discovering and listing all the writer s works (published and unpublished) and all the significant extant forms of these works (including manuscripts and typescripts), such an editor is unlikely to have the time, inclination, or training to assemble all those forms of all those works, to study them, and then to do the further research which would, finally, enable him to determine the scope and to establish the basic editorial procedure for any collected edition which would not soon require to be done over again.[4]

The second factor involves the textual standards of the edition. No commercial publisher is likely to endorse, no commercial editor is likely to prepare, a text which is adequately made by even the minimal standards of today - that is, one based upon the accurate collation of all relevant forms of the text, with significant variants accounted for, and the best copy-text chosen and sensibly emended in the light of the available evidence. Even if such a text were prepared for them by other hands, commercial publishers in this country have so far been unwilling to abandon their usual house-styling and to permit an author his own stylistic innovations and irregularities, the archaisms and innovations of spelling and punctuation and grammar which are almost always features of our works of literature, but which are almost never recognized by our manuals of style.

Finally, even if a comprehensive edition were well planned, and the text for it properly prepared, practical experience teaches us the sad lesson that, under the present

4 / The handling of the short stories of Fitzgerald and Hemingway by Scribners, and of Faulkner by Random House, illustrates this point. In all three cases the publisher failed to solve most of the problems inherent in discovering what stories the author had written; in planning ahead to determine what would be the best groupings for them for selective or comprehensive publication in book form; and in determining whether or not there were textual problems that required more attention than the simple copy-editing of a previous book or magazine text.

conditions of commercial publishing, it would be nearly impossible to produce it. This third factor has often been overlooked (even by the publishers and editors of scholarly editions), but it can hardly be stressed too strongly that to print a definitive text of any length requires an enormously expensive and long drawn-out proofreading process, with an absolute hands-off policy enforced upon editors, designers, printers, and proofreaders who are, from long habit, and quite properly, accustomed to normalize, and regularize, and modernize the typescripts and proofsheets which pass through their hands.

The present state of the Faulkner text, then, is unsatisfactory, but entirely understandable, granted the fact that his work is for the most part still in copyright. And I must emphasize that not only does this situation not distinguish him from his contemporaries among American novelists, it does not distinguish him from his forebears. Hawthorne and Melville, Twain and Howells and Crane in their time suffered from inconsistent and unintelligent house-styling, from copy-editing that significantly altered the texture of their prose, from inept proof-reading, and from a lack of intelligent planning in the publication of collected editions when such editions were commercially feasible. What does distinguish the situation in the contemporary field, however, from that of our nineteenth-century authors, is the strong and growing pressure which now exists to bring out better editions of literary works while they are still in copyright. And along with this pressure we have the availability of the materials necessary for making better editions, and of the scholars capable of using such materials for such a purpose. Our need and our desire for good texts of near-contemporary works grow with almost dizzying speed. Increasingly sophisticated critical attention is being paid to the literary works of our own century, precisely when standards of editing are being raised to new levels, and when new techniques are making possible increased fidelity to an author's intentions. Another contemporary phenomenon is the survival of a far higher percentage than ever before of the documents upon which these better texts must rest; today manuscripts and proofsheets, editorial correspondence, and even manufacturing records find their way quickly into collections which are available to scholars. In consequence, it is not surprising that the difference between the texts which we have now, and those which we need and might have (and later generations will have), becomes increasingly obvious, and increasingly irksome.

The problem, then, is one of control - control by commercial publishers who for a host of reasons are unlikely to see eye to eye with literary scholars concerning the nature of a definitive text. And this, I must emphasize, is just as it should be. Academic critics are not always ready to admit it, but it seems to me not only understandable but wholly proper that commercial publishers should differ with us concerning the production of literary texts; for if they were accustomed to doing things our way, they would shortly go out of business, and without commercial publishers there would be no professional writers, and very little literature, at least in the field of fiction. Further, I am inclined to think that as many literary texts have been poorly prepared by professional scholars, and published by university presses, as have been corrupted by the commercial publishing process.

Nevertheless, in a world where definitive literary texts are, at least occasionally, prepared and seen through the press, there is an ideal and a standard; and the greater the author, and the more attention he receives from the scholarly world, the greater will be the agitation for texts commensurate with the significance of his work.

Let me, then, agitate a little. First I am going to describe what seems to me an ideal Faulkner edition, one for which there would be ample time, money, and scholarly energy available to do the job right. In outlining this edition I shall be indulging in a form of scholarly day-dreaming, imagining a world in which there are no problems of access to papers, no bothersome copyright difficulties, no illegible words in manuscripts. Then, descending from the ideal to the practicable, I am going to propose specifically what I believe can be done at the present time, and under the present circumstances, to make available the best possible text of Faulkner.

THE IDEAL EDITION: A DEFINITIVE TEXT

In that ideal world which will one day exist for Faulkner studies, we may believe, the surviving documents which must be the foundation of his text will all have been collected and made available. Every scrap of manuscript, typescript, and proofsheet will have been found, and will have been placed in one of only a few major collections (to aid collation and cut down on travel costs). Furthermore, this task will have been accomplished sufficiently soon for all necessary supporting evidence to be obtained - by interviewing editors and agents before they die, by checking manufacturing records before they are destroyed. Painstaking biographical research will have shown whether or not Faulkner was able to read proof on certain works, will show what authors he read, and even in what editions he read them. Linguistic studies of considerable depth and breadth will have been completed, showing what dialect forms existed in Faulkner's time and place, and enabling an editor to distinguish between a typing error and a new way of recording an uncommon pronunciation.

Not only will there be definitive dialect atlases and historical dictionaries, there will be concordances - although it must be admitted, if regretfully, that even in an ideal world it is too much to expect a complete and accurate concordance as a working tool in the preparation of a definitive edition, for such a concordance can only be based upon the completed text of that edition. No, the editorial work of the definitive edition must begin with an unsatisfactory concordance based upon existing, defective texts, although parts of the concordance can be progressively updated as each volume of the edition is completed.

To bring about so ideal a state of affairs for a Faulkner edition, a great deal of time will obviously be necessary: time to multiply the number of persons who stumble upon previously unknown Faulkner items in obscure periodicals, time for complete files of small-town newspapers to make their way from attics to libraries, time for selfish collectors to die and their generous heirs to give (or even their penurious heirs to sell) their manuscripts to public collections; time to produce the well-trained scholars who will do all that basic bibliographical, biographical, and linguistic research upon Faulkner, and to produce those other scholars whose general studies of printing and publishing procedures in Faulkner's time, or whose editions of other authors, will show the way toward the accomplishment of a definitive Faulkner text.

This millennium, I suspect, will never come to pass; no matter how long we wait to undertake the 'definitive' Faulkner edition, and no matter how industrious is our research in the meantime, some editorial problems will be insoluble, or rather, legitimate disagreement will still be possible concerning them. In the last analysis, it will be impossible to determine whether Faulkner or an editor is responsible for various changes made between typescript and printed form of certain works, impossible to be sure that an apparent misprint is not an intentional coinage. Nevertheless, after the lapse of another quarter-century or so, it ought to be possible to publish a Faulkner text as good as the new editions of Hawthorne, Melville, Howells, and Crane, which are now being produced under the sponsorship of the CEAA and which have set new textual standards for the editing of novelists in English.[5] If it were not for the problem of copyright control, such an edition of

5 / Fredson Bowers and Matthew Bruccoli were responsible for the text and apparatus of the Centenary Edition of the four volumes of Hawthorne's novels, published 1962-8 by the Ohio State University Press.

Faulkner could probably be produced not only according to the standards, but under the sponsorship of the CEAA - that is, with the editorial expenses of the volumes subsidized by the CEAA rather than by the publisher. (Although the CEAA has for several years been interested in undertaking editions of our most important twentieth-century novelists, no such project has proved feasible.)

Let us suppose, though, that a CEAA edition of Faulkner were to be produced now. The format of the volumes would undoubtedly follow that of the other CEAA editions of prose fiction. Each volume would include both the established text and, separately, the textual apparatus. No textual notes, or even superscript numbers referring the reader to such notes, would clutter the text of the fiction. According to CEAA practice, once these volumes had been published, the text alone could be brought out, perhaps in paperback, making it available to the general reader who would not be interested in the compendious tables of variants, lists of emendations, and other scholarly paraphernalia which were necessary to establish the text (and which would still be available to scholars, of course, in the original CEAA edition). Even if no such general supervisory and funding organization as the CEAA exists, once Faulkner's major works are out of copyright I think we may assume that the format of the volumes of a definitive edition, when eventually it is published, is likely to prove quite similar to the format with which we are becoming familiar in the CEAA editions now in progress.

THE PRACTICABLE EDITION: A DEFINITIVE APPARATUS

Although at present a collected Faulkner edition made according to CEAA standards seems, then, impossible as long as his major works are in copyright, I am nevertheless convinced that nearly all his works can be 'edited,' if I may stretch the definition of the term slightly, independently of his commercial publishers, and according to the highest textual standards. The solution to the problem lies, I believe, in carrying one step further the separation of apparatus and text already permitted when reprint publishers are allowed to reproduce a CEAA text without its apparatus. In brief, I propose to prepare and publish the apparatus for definitive texts of at least some of Faulkner's books, keyed to the already existing commercial texts by the usual page-line references. The careful critic or student would continue to use the best available printed text - the original American editions, most of which are still available, either from Random House or in Modern Library or Vintage reissues. But, knowing the imperfections of this text, the careful student or critic would check it against the list of corrections and emendations in the published apparatus for the book, which would be available in some learned journal. Before publishing an article or writing a term-paper, he would check his quotations against the apparatus; better yet, he would use the apparatus as a sort of edit-it-yourself kit, going through his book text and correcting it by hand.

For nearly all of Faulkner's novels it would be possible to produce such an apparatus and to publish it now. For some of them - *As I Lay Dying* is an example - the apparatus would be minimal, the original published text having been faithfully edited and proofread. For others the apparatus would be more bulky and cumbersome to use; an example is *Absalom, Absalom!*, of which the original typescript was comparatively flawed, and which was ineptly copy-edited and proofread.

There is no reason why the textual research for such an 'edition' of Faulkner's novels could not be done now. All published texts, and surviving manuscript, typescript, and proof versions could be collated, variants recorded, supporting evidence studied, the text established, and the apparatus published. Ideally the task would be done one book at a time, and over a period of years, so that the research for each novel would have a maximum value for those that followed. And if in the meantime further evidence turned up which affected an already 'edited' text - a manuscript that had been presumed lost, some editorial correspondence - it would be a relatively simple and inexpensive process to publish a supplement to the existing apparatus, or even to bring out a new edition of it. Ultimately all the apparatus could be brought out together; a rough calculation indicates that the apparatus for all Faulkner's novels except *Sartoris* could be published in two or three volumes.

The basic difference between the CEAA Faulkner that I am proposing, then, and the CEAA novel texts that we already have, would be the complete physical separation of the apparatus from the text. But we should not underestimate the significance of this difference. In the CEAA Hawthorne, for example, errors are corrected and emendations are made in the text, these changes being recorded and explained in the apparatus. The text itself is reliable. For Faulkner, the text would remain what it is: possibly reliable, possibly not. The apparatus would bear the burden of correction as well as explanation, and would become more awkward to use as the textual problems became more complex.

The only major difficulty that such an 'edition' must overcome is that of obtaining permission from an author, or his estate, to quote from unpublished manuscripts and typescripts.[6]

The first novel that I propose to 'edit' according to this plan is *Go Down, Moses,* which was originally published in 1942 by Random House. It was several times reprinted without textual change, and in 1955 was reissued (still unchanged), in the Modern Library series. The work is important, and the original text is widely available, then; and,

6 / I am grateful to Mrs Jill Faulkner Summers, Faulkner's daughter and literary executrix, for approving this project and giving permission to quote from unpublished portions of manuscripts and typescripts. I am further indebted to her, and to Professors Cleanth Brooks and Michael Millgate, for consenting to serve as an advisory editorial board for this edition.

further to recommend it as the first volume in this 'edition,' the text is badly in need of correction at many points. Faulkner's typescript was sometimes a sloppy one; it was quite badly copy-edited; there is no evidence that the author saw proofs, and the proofreading and printing of the volume were poorly done. Fortunately, the evidence survives, among Faulkner's papers, to solve virtually all of the textual problems of the novel, and I give a few examples here of those problems and their solutions.

In chapter four, 'The Old People,' there is a somewhat puzzling reference to a hunter encountering 'somebody's straw cow' in a thicket.[7] Perhaps this phrase has always been taken to refer to the colour of the animal; or possibly the critics have assumed some sort of elaborate aspersion upon the poor creature, along the lines of straw men; but an early typescript reveals that Faulkner wrote 'stray cow' – making the error in his final version.

The dialogue of the novel sometimes presents problems even when the text is correct, particularly when the emotional stress of a character is signalled by a certain turgidity of language. But there is nothing to be gained from assuming that one of the hunters, Will Legate, is upset or confused in the sixth chapter, 'Delta Autumn,' when he says the following:

> '... Well, I wouldn't say that Roth Edmonds can hunt one doe every day and night for two weeks and was a poor hunter or a unlucky one neither. A man that still have the same doe left to hunt on again next year -' (p. 346)

This is a simple printer's error: the transposition of the second and third lines of the speech. But it is a little surprising that the error has never been caught and corrected in any reprinting of the original edition of the book, or

7 / *Go Down, Moses* (New York 1942) 185. Subsequent references in the text, by page number, are to this edition. For permission to refer to the original typescript readings here I am grateful to Mrs Jill Faulkner Summers.

even in any of the many separate versions of this chapter, in anthologies and textbooks, which I have examined.

The same chapter contains, in the book and all other printed versions I have seen, the somewhat alarming description of the delta country as having 'mile-wide parallelograms wrought by ditching the dyking machinery' (p. 342). Apparently no one who was concerned with the text of this chapter, either in its original edition or later, seems to have been given pause by the thought that one would have to ditch quite a lot of dyking machinery to make a parallelogram a mile wide; but the typescript reads, obviously, that the parallelograms were made 'by ditching and dyking machinery'.

These are simple printer's errors that should have been caught in the proofreading process and can be easily corrected by reference to Faulkner's typescript. Another category of textual error is not so easy to detect or to correct. These are errors due to flaws in the typescript itself, which made their way into the book text uncorrected. An example from the second chapter, 'The Fire and the Hearth,' appears in a description of Lucas Beauchamp's moonshining activities. Reference is made to the time when he 'fired up for his first fun not a mile from Zack Edmonds' kitchen door' (p. 35). The word 'fun' seems a little puzzling; Lucas is not distilling whiskey for the fun of it. But the typescript reading is identical. The correct reading, however, appears in an earlier draft of the passage, where the word is 'run'.

A more complicated problem from the same chapter appears in a description of a creek in flood. Ten days' rain had brought 'the creek out of banks until the whole valley rose, bled a river choked with down timber and drowned livestock' (p. 45). The image of the flooded valley bleeding a river seems singularly inappropriate and the sentence is awkward. Faulkner's typescript, at the crucial point, reads 'rese,bled' instead of the 'rose, bled' of the printed book, and no surviving earlier version contains this passage. But the difficuly is cleared up by assuming that the typescript's 'rese,bled' is a simple typing error in which a comma was struck for the key next to it, and that Faulkner meant to type 'resembled'. Presumably, since the typescript was not changed, either the printer emended 'rese' to 'rose' or the change was made in proof, and not by Faulkner.

And there is a category of errors which result from editorial tampering. A few examples from the first chapter, 'Was,' will suffice. There the narrative centres upon a nine-year-old boy, born in 1850 on a farm in northern Mississippi, and obviously somewhat short of formal education. His language is appropriately colloquial - or was until a schoolmarmish copy-editor improved some of it. The editorial hand is obvious, in the typescript, where it changed the boy's 'Only it didn't seem like they were going to eat' to 'Only it didn't seem as if they were going to eat' (p. 9); changed 'glare at one another' to 'glare at each other' (p. 17); and reunited a number of the youngster's split infinitives. One could wish that this editor, instead of educating that little boy and making him speak more formally, had corrected the book proofs more carefully.

Making available, by means of a published apparatus, a corrected text of *Go Down, Moses* might be expected, eventually, to have some effect upon the presently published text of the novel.[8] But we must assume that whenever a new edition is brought out, house-styling and copy-editing are likely to produce further errors, even if the attempt is made to correct the old ones. And it is illuminating and disturbing to recall that although Matthew Bruccoli brought out in a bibliographical journal nearly six years ago his 'Material for a Centenary Edition of *Tender is the Night,*' which established the text of that Fitzgerald novel in the same fashion, and for the same reason, that I

8 / Some years ago I proposed to Random House that they bring out a new edition of *Go Down, Moses*, with a corrected text, which I offered to supply and see through the press for them. The offer was not accepted.

am proposing now to edit Faulkner, the article has apparently had no effect whatever.[9]

Let me conclude with a few remarks about other possible applications of this method of establishing texts. Although, as proposed here, it is designed to overcome the problem of the control of a literary text by a publisher unwilling or unable to devote the time and money to correcting it, obviously this method would have significant uses in areas where there is no such problem of control. There are many out-of-copyright literary works which are badly in need of a better text, but which are unlikely to receive the financial support that would make possible a new letterpress edition. In such a case, the apparatus could be generated and keyed to the existing text, just as I have proposed for Faulkner, on the assumption that there are sufficient copies of that text around for the critic and scholar to consult. It would be a simple matter to publish the apparatus in a journal, identifying copies, in a few principal libraries, of the particular edition and impression to which the apparatus was keyed. Only a short step beyond this would be to state, in the apparatus, which library or libraries would supply a Xerox or microfilm of the particular text the apparatus was keyed to. A further step would be the production, perhaps in microfiche, by one of the publishers which specializes in such reissues, of the original text - which might be sold with the apparatus (reproduced from its printed form in the learned journal) included as an appendix. A further refinement would be to make the apparatus available only with the microfiche (or Xerox or microfilm or whatever) reissue of the text. An even further reduction in expense would be, for this last method, to reproduce the apparatus from typescript rather than letterpress.

9 / *Studies in Bibliography* 17 (1964) 177-93. Not only has the article been ignored by the publisher of the faulty text of the novel, Scribners, but the textual scholars who should have been following up Professor Bruccoli's pioneering example have yet to be heard from. And the article is not even mentioned in a recent survey of Fitzgerald criticism and scholarship in Bryer, ed., *Fifteen Modern American Authors.*

A complete (definitive) edition of a minor author could be published by this method, its text established through the apparatus, with a minimum of expenditure of time and money. The same saving of scholars' time could be effected by reproducing the original texts full-size by offset, with the apparatus appended, as in the microfiche reissue. Or a combination of offset and microfiche publication might prove practicable, the publisher inviting subscriptions to both series.

In short, the separation of apparatus from text, and the keying of a new apparatus to an old or existing text, offer in combination a wide variety of opportunities to the resourceful editor and publisher of literary texts. Nor should the opportunities of such editing in doctoral dissertations be ignored. As printing costs go up, and as our major authors are taken care of in definitive letterpress editions, procedures such as these, or further variations upon them, are likely to prove more and more attractive. And, ultimately, the Center for Editions of American Authors may find it expedient to subsidize the research for such an edition - the practicable text and the definitive apparatus - and to grant the CEAA seal of approval to the apparatus, rather than to the text, at an enormous saving of scholars' time and publishers' money.[10]

10 / A year after this paper was read, it became possible for such a textual apparatus as is described here to be approved by the CEAA. At its meeting on 27 December, 1970, in New York, the CEAA Executive Committee agreed that a second seal might be awarded, with the wording 'An Approved Textual Apparatus' instead of 'An Approved Text.'

‘A Might Collation’ Animadversions on the Text of F. Scott Fitzgerald

MATTHEW J. BRUCCOLI

The title for this paper is taken from a typo in the first printing of the Scribner Library edition of *Tender is the Night* (A-1.60[C]) - where ‘might collation’ should read ‘mighty collation.’ The variant exemplifies the condition of Fitzgerald’s editions - a series of ‘might collations.’ That is, a series of collations that might have been performed; or, when performed, collations that might have been used by editors.

In the case of F. Scott Fitzgerald we have the paradoxical combination of a great stylist and a wretched speller and punctuator, a craftsman who was careless about details. Fitzgerald’s attitude toward his proofs is symptomatic of the whole textual problem he presents: he tended to regard proofs as a special kind of typescript. He laboriously worked over them - but he was revising, not correcting. A representative Fitzgerald proof - say for *The Great Gatsby* or *Tender is the Night* - is so heavily revised that no compositor or copy-editor could produce perfect proof revises from it. A further complication comes from the role of Maxwell Perkins, who seems to have exercised special responsibility for Fitzgerald’s proofs, but who, like Fitzgerald, does not appear to have been greatly concerned with details. The other side of the case is that a superb archive of Fitzgerald's manuscripts, typescripts, proofs, and even marked copies of the books survives at Princeton. Yet we have sloppy texts, although the material for definitive editions - or at very least corrected and improved texts - is available. For Fitzgerald's two masterpieces - *Gatsby* and *Tender is the Night* - usable work has been made available by scholars, but has not been used by Scribners.

The text of *The Great Gatsby* was the subject of an article in 1958, Bruce Harkness' 'Bibliography and the Novelistic Fallacy.'[1] Professor Harkness demonstrated that the crucial edition in the transmission of the *Gatsby* text is Edmund Wilson's 1941 edition of *The Last Tycoon*, which included *Gatsby*. The Wilson text has 136 departures from the 1925 first edition - plus the emendation of 'Wolfshiem' to 'Wolfsheim' throughout. Of these 136 variants, some 25 are substantives. In addition, Mr Wilson omitted the epigraph poem and the dedication. In 1953 Malcolm Cowley undertook to revise the plates of the Wilson edition of *Gatsby* for the Scribner *Three Novels* collection. The Cowley text is not a new edition in that the type for the novel was not reset; Mr Cowley emended the 1941 Wilson plates in 62 spots. Of these 62 alterations, 39 are substantives. The importance of Mr Cowley's text is that it includes 39 revisions out of 41 in Fitzgerald's own marked copy of *Gatsby*. It is baffling that nowhere does the Cowley text indicate that it incorporates the author's own revisions - much less list these authorized emendations. (See appendix I to this article.)

The most widely distributed text of *Gatsby* is the 1957 'Student's Edition' - since incorporated into the Scribner Library series. Copy-text for this new edition was the 1953 Cowley revision of the 1941 Wilson edition. The 'Student's Edition' has 193 departures from the 1925 first edition - plus the 'Wolfsheims' - of which 67 are substantives. It omits 19 words at one point and a 4-word sentence at

1 / *Studies in Bibliography* 12 (1958); revised for *Bibliography and Textual Criticism,* ed. O M Brack, Jr, and Warren Barnes (Chicago: University of Chicago Press 1969)

another point; most important, it deletes 6 section breaks indicating time changes in the novel. I trust that the effect of these suppressions of chronological signals on the complex structure of *Gatsby* requires no analysis here.

On the basis of the attention Professor Harkness' article received in the scholarly community, one would have expected it to have resulted in an improved text of *The Great Gatsby*. It has not. There were 16 printings from the Student's Edition plates through 1969: a collation of the first and sixteenth printings reveals 47 variants (31 substantives), of which 5 are rejections of revisions Fitzgerald made in his own copy. These 47 plate alterations first appear in the H printing of 1963; but none is in the J printing of 1965, presumably printed from a set of duplicate plates. The alterations are in the current 1969 P printing. (See appendix II to this article.)

All printings of all Scribners editions of *Gatsby* beginning with *The Last Tycoon* have emended first printing 'orgastic' to 'orgiastic' in Nick's closing oration: 'Gatsby believed in the green light, the orgastic future that year by year recedes before us.' The *i* is inserted in the margin of Fitzgerald's copy, but I am not certain that this emendation was Fitzgerald's. Since Edmund Wilson did not use Fitzgerald's copy in 1941 - it may not have been available to him - his emendation could only have been a guess. That Scott Fitzgerald knew the difference between 'orgastic' and 'orgiastic' and used 'orgastic' deliberately is proved by his January 1925 letter to Maxwell Perkins responding to Perkins' proof queries: '"Orgastic" is the adjective for "orgasm" and it expresses exactly the intended ecstasy. It's not a bit dirty.'[2] Yet all Scribners editions in print read 'orgiastic.' Only the London Folio Society and English Penguin editions preserve 'orgastic.' My point is that, thirteen years after 'Bibliography and the Novelistic Fallacy,' its effect on the text of *Gatsby* is negligible. The only evidence that anyone connected with the publication

2 / *The Letters of F. Scott Fitzgerald*, ed. Andrew Turnbull (New York: Scribners, 1963) 175. See Jennifer E. Atkinson, 'Fitzgerald's marked copy of *The Great Gatsby*,' *Fitzgerald / Hemingway Annual 1970*

of *Gatsby* used the article is the 'correction' of the plates of the Student's Edition - but the fact that this correction conceals 5 readings that have Fitzgerald's authority indicates that whoever tried to use Professor Harkness' article simply didn't know what to do with it. This unknown editor seems to have checked - collated is probably too strong - the Student's Edition against either the 1925 first edition or *The Last Tycoon* volume, but then didn't know what to do: so he corrected some obvious typos, restored the 6 section breaks, and for some reason rejected 5 of Fitzgerald's revisions while retaining some 30 others. Then, after this work was done, the alterations were not made in the duplicate plates.

That Scribners has no trained textual men on its staff is not surprising; that they have never brought in a textual consultant to vet *Gatsby* is not especially surprising - but that they have failed to capitalize on the fact that their Scribner Library textbook edition includes some revision from Fitzgerald's own copy is puzzling. Surely they could have made pedagogical, as well as promotional, hay out of a list of the author's revisions. Yet nowhere does any Scribners edition of *Gatsby* even mention that Fitzgerald's copy has been consulted.

The material for a definitive edition of *Gatsby* exists: the manuscript and the revised proofs are available at Princeton and I have a set of the unrevised galleys. One can understand a commercial publisher's reluctance to endow a definitive edition. But an accurate 'practical' edition of *Gatsby* could be prepared in twenty-four hours.

I have heard it said that Professor Harkness' article failed to influence the text of *Gatsby* because it did not supply collations and a list of emendations. That sounds reasonable, but the case of *Tender is the Night* indicates otherwise. In 1964 I published 'Material for a Centenary Edition of *Tender is the Night*.'[3] I naively thought that this do-it-yourself kit would produce a good edition of *Tender*: my article included a list of 274 emendations to

3 / *Studies in Bibliography* 17 (1964)

be made in the first-edition copy-text, textual notes on the emendations, a historical collation, and a list of revisions Fitzgerald made in his copy of the novel. The results of this article - which I confess was intended to be the first of a series of do-it-yourself editorial kits - were about the same as for Professor Harkness' article, even though I included the nails, paint, and glue. I indicated that 161 readings in the 1960 Scribner Library edition of *Tender* required editorial attention. But between the 1960 first printing and the 1967 twelfth printing only 14 alterations were made in the plates. Of these 14 plate changes, 9 correct typos, 2 correct punctuation, 1 corrects the spelling of a place name, and 1 introduces a fresh typo (appendix III to this article.)

There is more than spelling, grammar, and punctuation at stake, for *Tender is the Night* has chronological problems which seriously affect the reader's reaction to the novel. Some difficulty is caused by the inconsistencies in the ages of the characters; and Fitzgerald's inattention to the time-span of his story confuses Book III, which traces Dick's crack-up and which several critics have found unsatisfactory. It is essential that the reader be aware of the pace of Dick's collapse, but from the first edition it is hard to tell whether Book III occupies one or two years. We know from Fitzgerald's preliminary plan that the novel opens with Rosemary's arrival on the Riviera in June 1925 and ends with Dick's departure from the Riviera in July 1929.[4] Fitzgerald seems to have confused four years with five summers. Thus, on page 276 of the first printing he gives the year of Dick's Rome meeting with Rosemary as 1928, but on this page and on page 277 he adds an extra year to their ages. If the break-up of the Divers' marriage and Dick's abdication are to occur in the summer of 1929, then Book III occupies one year. At this point four years

4 / Fitzgerald's 'General Plan' is with the manuscript of *Tender is the Night* at the Princeton University Library. It contains contradictory information about the time-span of the novel. The ages of Dick and Nicole are reckoned in four- and five-year spans and the ages of Rosemary and Tommy only in five-year spans. In two places Fitzgerald states that the story ends in July 1929.

(but five summers) have passed since Rosemary and Dick first met - not five years, as Fitzgerald states on page 364. That this is the summer of 1929 gives Dick's crack-up an ironic significance in view of what will happen on Wall Street in October. Unfortunately, Fitzgerald's carelessness or confusion blurred this effect. Indeed, Cowley is convinced that Fitzgerald changed the time-scheme of the novel after he drew up the preliminary plan, and that *Tender is the Night* does in fact cover five years:

> We will be told several times that five years have passed since Rosemary's first visit to the Cap d'Antibes in the summer of 1925. Her second visit, then, was in June, 1930. The date reveals a change in Fitzgerald's plans ... There is always a sense of historical events in the background of the novel ... and many episodes in it have the color of a special year. At this point, however, the author needed more elapsed time to accomplish Dick's ruin - five years instead of four - and actually 1930 was better for the historical background than 1929. It was the year when, in spite of the crash, there were more rich Americans in Europe than ever before and when the summer season on the Riviera was the biggest and maddest.[5]

Although Cowley does not account for the year 1929, his idea is supported by Fitzgerald's statement at the beginning of chapter four of Book III that 'The Villa Diana had been rented again for the summer ...' which indicates that a full year passes between the Divers' departure from the clinic and their return to the Riviera. But my feeling is that this detail is another piece of Fitzgerald's own carelessness, of which there is ample evidence in the novel. The case for the four-year time-span rests on two points: it is extremely unlikely that Fitzgerald would not have mentioned the Crash if it had occurred during the novel; and Tommy's statement on page 353 that his stocks are doing well hardly belongs to the summer of 1930. Nevertheless, I own a Fitzgerald inscription - reportedly torn out of a copy of *Tender is the Night* - that reads: 'F. Scott Fitz-

5 / *Tender is the Night,* 'The Author's Final Version' (New York: Scribners, 1951) 355

gerald requests the pleasure of Laura Guthrie's company in Europe 1917-1930.'

I do agree with Cowley's comment that the year 1926 is unaccounted for in the action of the first edition. The trip to Gstaad occurs during the December of 1925, and in chapter fourteen of Book II Fitzgerald states that Dick has been at the clinic for eighteen months, which would make the time of this chapter June 1927. But the Rome chapters that follow are specifically dated 1928, and one year must be accounted for. Cowley suggests that the Divers remained on the Riviera during 1926 while the clinic was being renovated. However, it is possible that December 1925 is where Fitzgerald lost track of his time-scheme. If the Rome chapters are moved back to 1927, then Cowley can have his two years for Book III and I can have my pre-Crash conclusion.

My teaching of *Tender is the Night* has convinced me that the chronological problems - not the flashback structure - puzzle my students. That the novel opens in 1925, has a flashback to 1917-19, and then has a bridge to 1925 presents no real difficulty. What troubles students - and baffles some - is that after 1925 they can't tell what year they are in or how much time has elapsed since the opening of the novel. *Tender is the Night* is Dick Diver's novel: the reader who cannot calculate the velocity of Dick's dive loses much of the meaning of the novel. An edition of *Tender* that fixed the chronology might give this novel a fitter audience.

The Last Tycoon presents a special case. It was edited for publication in 1941, after Fitzgerald's death, by Edmund Wilson. Given Mr Wilson's approach to editing, *The Last Tycoon* is a surprisingly conservative edition. Mr Wilson identified Fitzgerald's latest drafts and mostly confined himself to copy-editing them. There was no serious rewriting by the editor. In one place, however, Wilson made some inexplicably bad emendations. In chapter four where Pete Zavras the cameraman is thanking Monroe Stahr for having scotched the rumour that he is going blind, Fitzgerald's typescript reads: 'You are the Aeschylus and Diocanes of the moving picture ... Also the Esculpias and the Minanorus.' This passage is emended in Wilson's hand to: 'You are the Aeschylus and the Euripides of the moving picture ... Also the Aristophanes and the Menander.' Wilson's confidence in his own erudition betrayed him. 'Diocanes' surely indicates that Fitzgerald was trying to write 'Diogenes' - not 'Euripides.' One might be inclined to argue that Fitzgerald was simply listing names from classical civilization for their sound with no deliberate selection; but the emendation of 'Esculpias' to 'Aristophanes' destroys the point of Zavras' compliment. Surely 'Esculpias' was Fitzgerald's spelling for 'Esculpius,' the god of medicine and healing. Since Stahr has discovered that there is nothing wrong with Zavras' eyesight, he deserves to be called 'Esculapius' - not 'Aristophanes'. Sometimes uneducated authors know better than learned editors.[6]

The main problem with the Wilson edition of *The Last Tycoon* - which is the only edition of the work - is that it makes the unfinished novel seem more finished than it was at Fitzgerald's death. *The Last Tycoon* is a fragment and should be read and judged as such. Edmund Wilson's Foreword notes: 'The text which is given here is a draft made by the author after considerable rewriting; but it is by no means a finished version. In the margins of almost every one of the episodes, Fitzgerald had written comments - a few of them are included in the notes - which expressed his dissatisfaction with them or indicated his ideas about revising them.'[7] Wilson then prints the first six chapters of the novel in what seems to be a very finished form indeed - with *a few* of Fitzgerald's comments included in the notes. Find them if you can. But Fitzgerald did not even complete six chapters. He left seventeen 'sections' or 'episodes' which Wilson has organized into chapters with no indication at all that these chapter divisions are not Fitzgerald's.

6 / 'Menander' doesn't seem to be a particularly good replacement for 'Minanorus'; perhaps Fitzgerald meant 'Mimnermus'.

7 / *The Last Tycoon* (New York: Scribners, 1941) ix

Wilson has made a sampling from the extensive body of Fitzgerald's notes without indicating the bulk of the material. Again, by this selecting and ordering Wilson has made *The Last Tycoon* seem neater, more disciplined, than it was. The full body of Fitzgerald's notes reveals that he had more material than he knew what to do with - that *The Last Tycoon* was gestating in much the same way as *Tender is the Night* did. I do not mean to suggest that Fitzgerald's notes indicate that he would not have been able to complete the novel. But they convince me that the novel, had Fitzgerald lived to publish it, would have been more elaborate than Wilson's edition of the material suggests. This prettying-up process by the editor is perhaps most clearly seen from the diagram of the 'Last Outline Made by the Author' as transcribed by Wilson. Printed in letterpress this diagram is convincing: it is carefully worked out in elaborate detail, and it is neat. The actual diagram is a palimpsest, not a roadmap, indicating that Fitzgerald was still working out his plot and structure. This diagram may be the 'Last Outline,' but it is not a final outline. Moreover, perhaps for reasons of modesty, Wilson omits from his diagram a note that is on Fitzgerald's outline: 'WRITTEN FOR TWO PEOPLE - FOR SF. AT 17 AND FOR EW AT 45 - IT MUST PLEASE THEM BOTH.'

Fitzgerald's published letters illustrate editorial atrocities. A sampling was first printed in *The Crack-Up* by Edmund Wilson in 1945, with this editorial note: 'In most of the letters of the first group [letters to friends], the spelling and punctuation have been left as they were in the originals, except for the uniform italicization of titles of books and magazines and the insertion of missing ends of parentheses.'[8] The note says nothing about the treatment of the second group, letters to Fitzgerald's daughter. But, from the implied distinction, one would assume that the letters to friends are uncut, but that some editing has been done on the letters to his daughter. There are leaders sprinkled through the letters of the first group, but since

8 / *The Crack-Up* (New York: New Directions, 1945) 243

Mr Wilson has not specified that these letters have been cut, the leaders could be Fitzgerald's own punctuation.

A collation of the *Crack-Up* letters against the texts in Andrew Turnbull's *The Letters of F. Scott Fitzgerald* reveals major omissions by Edmund Wilson. Here are samples: a paragraph omitted from the fall 1917 letter to Wilson; a sentence omitted from the 10 January 1918 letter to Wilson; a paragraph omitted from the 15 August 1919?/1920? letter to Wilson; most of a paragraph, plus 2 more paragraphs, plus 1 sentence omitted from the 25 November 1921 letter to Wilson; a paragraph omitted from 24 January 1922 letter to Wilson; a paragraph omitted from 25 June 1922 letter to Wilson; a paragraph omitted from 1 August 1922 letter to Wilson; 2 paragraphs omitted from 7 October 1924 letter to Wilson; a paragraph omitted from April 1925 letter to Bishop; 10 paragraphs omitted - with note - from February 1929 letter to Bishop; 28 words and postscript omitted from February 1933 letter to Wilson; 5 paragraphs omitted from September 1936 letter to Beatrice Dance with no indication; 3 sentences omitted from 16 May 1939 letter to Wilson; a paragraph omitted from 25 November 1940 letter to Wilson. In the letters to Frances Scott Fitzgerald, collation between *The Crack-Up* and *Letters* shows: postscript omitted from 8 August 1933 letter, without indication; two July 1939 letters scrambled by Wilson or Turnbull; 15 March 1940 letter scrambled by Wilson or Turnbull; 4 paragraphs and postscript omitted from 5 April 1939 letter without indication; 4 paragraphs omitted from 31 October 1939 letter without indication; sentence and paragraph omitted from 12 April 1940 letter without indication; 2 sentences and 2 paragraphs omitted from 27 April 1940 letter without indication; 5 sentences, plus paragraph, plus postscript omitted from 4 May 1940 letter without indication; 2 sentences and 2 paragraphs omitted from 7 May 1940 letter without indication; 3 paragraphs omitted from 11 May 1940 letter without indication; 9 paragraphs plus postscript omitted from 12 June 1940 letter without indication; 2 paragraphs plus postscript omitted from 15 June 1940 letter without indication; 5 paragraphs omitted from 20 June 1940 letter without indication. Enough.

By the way, in *The Crack-Up* Edmund Wilson reverses the titles of 'Pasting it Together' and 'Handle With Care.' This volume is the only American publication of the essays since their 1936 *Esquire* appearances; therefore for twenty-three years readers have thought that 'Pasting it Together' was 'Handle With Care' and that 'Handle With Care' was 'Pasting it Together.'

The foregoing list of omissions from *The Crack-Up* texts of Fitzgerald letters was, as I stated, based on collation with Turnbull's edition of the *Letters.* The opening of Turnbull's textual note explains, 'All omissions of words and sentences have been indicated by four dots since Fitzgerald sometimes used three dots as punctuation.'[9] This means that, as with Wilson, all the reader can tell from the appearance of four dots is that something is omitted; it is impossible for him to determine the extent of the omission. I have acquired some of the letters printed by Turnbull. In the letter of 22 December 1917 to Shane Leslie an 8-word marginal note is omitted, and the title Fitzgerald gives for his novel is changed from *The Romantic Egoist* to *Egotist*; in the 13 January 1919 letter to Leslie, Turnbull changes Fitzgerald's reaction to Father Fay's death from 'But selfishly I am sorry' to 'But selfishly dam sorry.' In five letters to Leslie there are some 130 silent emendations.

It would be too simple for me to draw the conclusion that I have all the virtue and Scribners has all the texts. Another conclusion can be drawn: textual scholars have done a lousy job of promoting their work. After all, if publishers do not believe in the value of good texts - indeed don't even understand what a good edition is - then we are not doing our job. We have failed to make people who use books and publish them understand why good texts matter; and we have failed to make them understand what a good text is and how it is edited. Publishers are not the only ones we are not getting to. Most teachers don't know anything

9 / *Letters*, xviii

about texts - and they don't care. Perhaps the teacher is the key figure. He picks the books for his classes. If enough teachers picked books on the basis of good texts, the publishers would respond. Apart from idealism, there is no special reason why a commercial publisher should respond to two articles in *Studies in Bibliography*. But publishers respond to book orders.[10]

A Fitzgerald editor can only publish his edition through Scribners - or with their permission. Therefore any edition of Fitzgerald - practical, definitive, or corrupt - must be a Scribners edition. But still I assert that Scribners is not the main culprit. If our colleagues don't know and don't care about good texts, why should a publisher? Piety to Fitzgerald and dedication to American literature are indeed blessed things. But can we expect publishers to be more scholarly than the scholars?

Copyright is short and literature is long. Most of the people reading this will be alive when Fitzgerald goes into public domain.[11]

POSTSCRIPT

The conference at which this paper was read took place in 1969, and some up-dating is required.

10 / The history of the Center for Editions of American Authors is instructive. That there is a CEAA sponsoring or supervising thirteen editions of American authors is miraculous. The fact that all volumes bearing the CEAA emblem must be made available to reprint publishers on a non-exclusive basis at a reasonable fee means that the CEAA is not in the business of producing expensive scholarly editions: the CEAA volumes are making inexpensive definitive editions available to everyone. But the support of the CEAA from the world of what Mencken called "beautiful letters" has been poor. Usually the CEAA editions have been given uncomprehending reviews in scholarly journals; in many cases they have received only brief-mention listings instead of reviews; they have received amateur abuse from Edmund Wilson; and an attempt to kill the CEAA has been made by a group within the profession who want the money to go into something "relevant." These people are not ignorant outsiders. They are ignorant insiders. We have little right to attack the publishers until we have educated our colleagues. To be sure, the case of Fitzgerald is different from the case of, say, Stephen Crane. Crane is in public domain. A scholar who edits a definitive edition of Crane can publish it and hope it will drive out bad editions.

11 / I gratefully acknowledge the help of Dr Jennifer Atkinson.

In 1970 a new edition (ie, a new setting of type) for *Gatsby* was included in *Fitzgerald's The Great Gatsby: The Novel, The Critics, The Background*, ed. Henry Dan Piper (New York: Scribners, 1970). Copy-text for this edition was the Scribner Library edition, which departs from the 1925 first printing in some 200 readings; this new setting introduces 25 new variants, of which 11 are substantives.[12]

Two new editions of Fitzgerald's letters are in press for fall-winter 1971 publication: *Dear Scott / Dear Max*, the Fitzgerald-Perkins correspondence, ed. Jackson Bryer and John Kuehl (New York: Scribners); and *As Ever, Scott Fitz,* the Fitzgerald-Ober correspondence, ed. Matthew J. Bruccoli and Jennifer McCabe Atkinson (New York / Philadelphia: Lippincott). These two collections represent different attempts to edit letters with fidelity to what the writer wrote. It appears that the next thrust in Fitzgerald scholarship will be concerned with sound editorial practice for his letters. The notion that his letters should be prettied-up for the sake of the so-called general reader is losing its adherents in the face of the growing recognition that the essential personal qualities of letters should be preserved when they are published. Fitzgerald's letters were not written for publication; therefore it is a distortion to silently alter them for publication.

I have located a note Fitzgerald wrote to a typist which says everything I've been trying to say: 'If you can manage it please get someone to read this with you – it's so important – and a few missing words would destroy so much.'

APPENDIXES

I
An Historical Collation: Scribners Editions of *The Great Gatsby*

12 / for collation see 'Editorial,' *Fitzgerald / Hemingway Annual 1970.* I hope that the pedigrees of editions in my *F. Scott Fitzgerald: A Descriptive Bibliography* (Pittsburgh: University of Pittsburgh Press, 1972) may help editors.

KEY

The first reading is that of the first printing, Scribners, April 1925

1925[2]	second printing, Scribners, August 1925
LT	*The Last Tycoon*, ed. Edmund Wilson, Scribners, 1941
TN	*Three Novels*, ed. Malcolm Cowley, Scribners, 1953
SE	Student's Edition, Scribners, 1957
FR	*Fitzgerald Reader*, ed. Arthur Mizener, Scribners, 1963
F	revision made by Fitzgerald in his copy of the first printing

HISTORICAL COLLATION

dedication	*omitted* LT, TN, FR
epigraph	*omitted* LT
1.6	criticising [criticizing TN, SE, FR
3.15	to-day [today FR
3.24	centre [center SE, FR
4.24	village [Village FR
5.15	Yale News [*Yale News* LT, TN, SE, FR
6.6	wonder [confusion F, TN, SE, FR
6.7	interesting [arresting F, TN, SE, FR
6.22	mansion [mansion, LT, TN, SE, FR
7.12	anti-climax [anticlimax LT, TN, SE, FR
7.16	away: [away; LT, TN, SE, FR
12.9	To-morrow [Tomorrow FR
12.18	room, [room. LT
15.18	evening too [evening, too, LT, TN, SE
16.3	'The ... Empires' [*The ... Empires* FR
17.6	leaned [learned LT, TN
17.10	to-night [tonight FR
18.21	I began [I said. F, TN, SE; I said: "This FR
19.21	startingly [startlingly LT, TN, SE, FR
21.28	contributary [contributory FR
22.6	Saturday Evening Post [*Saturday Evening Post* LT, TN, SE, FR
22.7	uninflected [uninfected LT, TN

23.5 you. [you? LT, TN, SE
23.7 night, [night LT, TN
23.10 fact [fact, LT, TN, SE
24.3 heart to heart [heart-to-heart LT, TN, SE
26.12 away, [way, SE
27.10 of ash-gray men [of men F, TN, SE
28.4 days, [days F, TN, SE, FR
28.15 cafes [restaurant F; restaurants, TN, SE, FR
28.20 afternoon, [afternoon TN, SE
30.10 her flesh [her surplus flesh F, TN, SE, FR
31.2; 31.27 news-stand [newsstand FR
31.27; 34.19 Town Tattle [*Town Tattle* LT, TN, SE, FR
32.1 Up-stairs [Upstairs FR
32.24 po*lice* [*police* SE
33.14-15 Avenue, warm ... afternoon. I [Avenue, so warm ... afternoon that I F, TN, SE, FR
34.20; 35.9 "Simon Called Peter" [*Simon Called Peter* LT, TN, SE, FR
35.8 had both disappeared [had disappeared F, TN, SE, FR
35.21 angle, [angle LT, TN, SE
37.4 appendicitus [appendicitis TN, SE
37.27 modelling [modeling FR
38.20 down-stairs [downstairs FR
38.22 'Montauk ... Gulls' [*Montauk ... Gulls* LT, TN, SE
38.23 'Montauk ... Sea' [*Montauk ... Sea* LT, TN, SE
38.27 too," [too?" LT, TN, SE, FR
40.1 'George ... Pump' [*George ... Pump* LT, TN, SE
41.6 gyped [gypped LT, TN, SE, FR
41.15 kyke [kike SE
42.12 I expected no affection [I had played no part in her past F, TN, SE, FR
42.17 out: 'Oh [out: She looked around to see who was listening. 'Oh F; out." She looked around to see who was listening. " 'Oh TN, SE, FR
43.2 park [Park SE
43.8 saw [was F, TN, SE, FR
44.17 the spot [the remains of spot F ⟨?⟩; the remains of the spot TN, SE; the remains of dried FR

44.25 face discussing, [face discussing LT; face, discussing TN, SE, FR
45.13 Town Tattle [*Town Tattle* LT, TN, SE, FR
45.29 Bridge . . . [Bridge . . . . LT, SE; Bridge . . . . . TN
46.3 Tribune [*Tribune* LT, TN, SE, FR
48.1 corps [crop SE
48.18 up-stairs [upstairs FR
48.21 bobbed [shorn F, TN, SE, FR
49.10 centre [center LT, TN, SE, FR
49.21 Follies [*Follies* LT, TN, SE
50.1-2 an amusement park [amusement parks F, FR
52.27 to-night [tonight LT, TN, SE, FR
54.10 rambling [rambling, LT, TN, SE
56.7 Claud [Claude LT, TN, SE
57.4; 57.12 finger-bowls [fingerbowls FR
57.8 Baker. [Baker, FR
57.19 First [3d F; Third TN, SE, FR
57.20 Twenty-eighth Infantry [9th Machine Gun Battalion F; ninth machine-gun battalion TN, SE, FR
57.22 Sixteenth [7th Infantry F; Seventy TN, SE, FR
58.22 eternal [external F, TN, SE, FR
58.29 Precisely ⟨circled in F⟩
59.1 rough-neck [roughneck LT, TN, SE, FR
59.7 himself [himself, LT, TN, SE
59.21 *you*'re [*you're* LT, TN, SE
60.16 chatter [echolalia 1925^2, LT, TN, SE, FR
60.19 Vladmir [Vladimir LT, TN, SE, FR
60.21 papers [papers, LT, TN, SE
60.26 'Vladmir ... World.' [Vladimir ... *World.* LT, TN, SE
61.8 "Jazz ... World" [*Jazz ... World* LT, TN, SE
61.9 over, [over FR
61.15 for [with TN, SE, FR
62.17 lyric again in [lyric in F ⟨? in margin⟩, TN, SE
63.20 to-night [tonight LT, TN, SE, FR
63.23 the [this SE, FR
64.29 to-morrow [tomorrow LT, TN, SE, FR
69.5 up-stairs [upstairs LT, TN, SE, FR
70.2 were lined five [were five F, TN, SE

70.3 theatre [theatre LT, TN, SE, FR
70.6-7 made unintelligible circles [outlined unintelligible gestures F, TN, SE, FR
70.13 every one [everyone LT, TN, SE, FR
70.20 house-party [house party FR
71.17 house party [house-party LT, TN, SE
73.13 time-table [timetable SE
75.12 Russel [Russell LT, TN, SE
75.14 Dewars [Dewers LT, TN, SE
76.19 to-day [today LT, TN, SE, FR
76.21 dashboard [running board FR
76.24 work in [work or rigid sitting in F, TN, SE, FR
77.4 sport?" [sport!" TN, SE
77.11 wind-shields [windshields FR
77.15 half a dozen [six ⟨circled in F⟩, TN, SE
79.17 the remains of my machine-gun battalion [two machine gun detachments F, TN, SE, FR
81.1 to-day [today LT, TN, SE, FR
83.29 sid [said LT, TN, SE
84.16 Metropole." [Metropole. F, TN, SE, FR
85.11 me [be SE
86.1 Gatsby, [Gatsby LT, TN, SE
91.2 sometime [some time LT, TN, SE, FR
91.22 armistice [Armistice LT, TN, SE
93.17 night [right LT, TN
94.23 children [little girls F ⟨?⟩, TN, SE, FR
94.26-29 "I'm ... creep - " [*"I'm ... creep - "* LT, TN, SE, FR
95.21 he's regular [he's a regular F, TN, SE, FR
96.23 busy [busy, TN, SE
98.15 taxi F note: ⟨His own car⟩
99.5 to-morrow [tomorrow LT, TN, SE, FR
99.13 to-morrow [tomorrow LT, TN, SE, FR
99.17 looked down at [looked at F, TN, SE, FR
100.3 didn't, [didn't LT, TN, SE
102.3 The Journal [*The Journal* LT, TN, SE, FR
102.9 asked. [asked LT, TN
102.15 "Economics," [*Economics,* LT, TN, SE, FR

107.2 craze, [craze LT, TN, SE
107.9 while willing, even eager [while occasionally willing F, TN, SE, FR
107.17 the large [a large F, TN, FR
108.8 hello, [hello LT, TN, SE
108.24 up-stairs [upstairs FR
109.21 *there*? [there? FR
110.7 out the door [out of the door LT, TN, SE, FR
110.10 Salons [salons FR
110.17 up-stairs [upstairs LT, TN, SE
110.20 bathrooms [bathrooms, LT, TN, SE
110.26 Adam's [Adam LT, TN, SE, FR
111.14 When [when TN, SE, FR
111.24 hulking patent cabinets [hulking cabinets FR
112.4 many colored [many-colored LT, TN, SE, FR
114.4 *quick!* [*quick*! LT, TN, SE
114.20 "sport shirt" [sport shirt TN, SE
114.26 up . . ." [up . . . ." TN, SE
115.1 downs-stairs [downstairs LT, TN, SE, FR
115.9 "The Love Nest" [*The Love Nest* LT, TN, SE
115.16-18 "In ... fun -" [*"In ... fun -"* LT, TN, SE, FR
115.23 hour [four LT
115.25 air. [air TN, SE
115.26-29 "One ... time -" [*"One ... time -"* LT, TN, SE, FR
116.13 can [will F, TN, SE, FR
117.25 Dakota, [Dakota LT, TN, SE, FR
118.22 seventeen year-old [seventeen-year-old LT, TN, SE; seventeen year old FR
119.21 College [college TN, SE, FR
119.22 St. Olaf's [St. Olaf FR
119.22 northern [southern LT, TN, SE, FR
120.11 property of [knowledge to F, TN, SE, FR
120.11 turgid journalism [turgid sub or suppressed journalism F, TN, SE; sub-journalism FR
120.25 pair [pairs TN, SE, FR
121.8 Boston and [Boston to do her stuff (?) and F
126.19 Gatsby [Gatsby. LT, TN, SE, FR
126.27 lady, [lady. FR

127.10 Oh [Oh, LT, TN, SE
127.11 Gatsby [Gatsby, LT, TN, SE
127.14 exclaimed, [exclaimed. LT, TN, SE, FR
128.23 to-morrow [tomorrow FR
130.25 they are [they're TN, SE, FR
131.6 rose [rose, LT, TN, SE, FR
131.23 "Three ... Morning," [*Three ... Morning,* LT, TN, SE
131.23 o'Clock [*O'Clock* LT, TN, SE, FR
136.16 to-morrow [tomorrow FR
138.15 centre [center FR
139.26 "The [The LT, TN
141.6 year. [year." LT, TN, SE
143.17 up-stairs [upstairs LT, TN, SE, FR
149.1 he had just [he just SE, FR
149.4 to-morrow [tomorrow FR
149.10 that other [that the other LT, TN, SE, FR
149.11 us with peculiar intensity from less [us less LT, TN, SE
153.9 Tennessee [Mississippi TN, SE
153.14 added. "There [added as if she might have sounded irreverent. "There F, TN, SE, FR
153.20 to-day [today LT, TN, SE, FR
154.21 voice, [voice LT, TN, SE
154.26 ice [ice, LT, TN, SE
155.3 -nineteen, [-nineteen. LT, TN, SE, FR
155.9 armistice [Armistice LT, TN, SE
155.26 row, [row. FR
157.21-24 know. I used ... know." [know." SE
158.9 more, [more LT, TN, SE
159.21 *too?* [*too?* LT, TN, SE
159.23 there're [there's FR
160.16 though," [though, FR
161.17 sport'!" [sport!' " FR
162.3 "killed a man" [killed a man FR
163.5 to-day's [today's LT, TN, SE, FR
163.6 birthday." [birthday. FR
163.20 wise [wise, LT

163.26 *break* [*end of page* LT, TN; *no break* SE
164.10 to-morrow [tomorrow FR
165.12 Mavromichaelis [Michaelis F, TN, SE, FR
165.16 it's [its LT, TN, SE, FR
165.25 ripped a little at [ripped at F, TN, SE, FR
165.29 away [away. LT, SE, FR
166.18 metal [wire F, TN, SE, FR
167.22 M-a-v [M-a-y LT, TN, SE
167.24 fiercely. [fiercely LT
167.25 "r-" ["r" LT, TN, SE, FR
169.3 him ... him, [him, ... him LT, TN, SE, FR
171.4 to-night [tonight FR
173.24 to-morrow [tomorrow LT, TN, SE, FR
174.11 down-stairs [downstairs LT, TN, SE, FR
176.24 inexplicable [enexplicable LT
177.28 intensity, [intensity LT, TN, SE, FR
178.2 up-stairs [upstairs LT, TN, SE, FR
178.5 lavender [lavender, LT, TN, SE
178.28 strata [stratum TN, SE, FR
180.24 armistice [Armistice LT, TN, SE
181.10 "Beale Street Blues" [*Beale Street Blues* LT, TN, SE
182.6 down-stairs [downstairs LT, TN, SE, FR
182.12 him." [him," LT, TN, SE
183.11 left [left, LT, TN, SE
183.18 with people [with the people SE, FR
184.7 to-day [today LT, TN, SE, FR
184.17 train, [train. LT, TN, SE, FR
187.22 Some one [Someone SE, FR
192.16 *break* [*end of page* LT, TN; *no break* SE
197.11 village [Village SE, FR
198.17 though [as F, TN, SE, FR
198.19 shocked [unmoved? F; unmoved TN, SE, FR
198.24 up-stairs [upstairs LT, TN, SE, FR
199.19 out. [out." LT
200.17 *break* [*no break* SE
201.15 Mr [Mr. SE, FR
202.4 up-stairs [upstairs LT, TN, SE, FR
203.9 to-morrow [tomorrow LT, TN, SE, FR

205.9 sick in tired [sickantired 1925[2], LT, TN, SE, FR
205.28 sid [said LT, TN, SE
207.11 that [that, LT, TN, SE
208.11 "Hopalong Cassidy." [*Hopalong Cassidy.* LT, TN, SE, FR
209.6-8 it?" / ¶ "It just shows you." / ¶ "Jimmy [it?" / ¶ "Jimmy LT, TN, SE
209.26 *break* [*no break* SE
211.7 Union Street Station [Union Station 1925[2], LT, TN, SE, FR
214.21 *break* [*no break* LT, TN, SE
215.17 up-stairs [upstairs LT, TN, SE, FR
216.16 *break* [*no break* SE
216.27 York [York, LT, TN, SE
218.12 orgastic [org/astic ⟨faint *i* in margin⟩ F; orgiastic LT, TN, SE, FR
218.14 to-morrow [tomorrow LT, TN, SE, FR
throughout Wolfshiem [Wolfsheim LT, TN, SE, FR

II

Collation of First (A-8.57) and Latest (P-9.69) Printings of the Student's Edition / Scribner Library Edition of *The Great Gatsby*

KEY

The first reading is that of the first printing. The following printings have been spot-checked: D-3.61; G-4.63; H-10.63; J-2.65; N8.68.

The fact that emendations which first appear in the H printing are not in the J printing but do appear in the N printing indicates the existence of duplicate plates.

18.8 off [off, H, N, P
23.8 of men [of ash-gray men H, J, N, P
24.13 afternoon [afternoon, H, N, P
26.6 office [office, H, N, P

27.27 *police* [po*lice* H, N, P
30.8 angle [angle, H, N, P
36.6 Park [park H, N, P
39.24 crop [corps H, N, P
41.16 an amusement park [amusement parks H, N, P
46.19 Claude [Claud H, N, P
50.9 papers, [papers H, N, P
51.26 lyric in [lyric again in H, N, P
55.27 as [at J, N, P
57.33 were five [were lined five H, N, P
57.33 taxicabs, bound for [taxicabs, for N, P
63.3 Russell [Russel H, N, P
63.4 Dewers [Dewars H, N, P
64.7 the dashboard [the running board H, N, P
64.27 six [half a dozen H, N, P
67.8 de Danilo [di Danilo H, N, P
70.10 said [sid H, N, P
71.17 be [me H, N, P
72.4 Gatsby [Gatsby, H, N, P
79.16 girls [girls, H, N, P
83.22 didn't [didn't, H, N, P
89.16 craze [craze, H, N, P
90.16 hello [hello, H, N, P
100.10 St. Olaf's [St. Olaf H, P
100.28 turgid sub or suppressed journalism [turgid sub-journalism H, P
106.11 particularly [peculiarly H, P
118.7 year." [year. H, P
123.7 spot [stop H, N, P
125.1 us less [us with peculiar intensity from less, H, N, P
128.12 Mississippi [Tennessee H, N, P
129.8 smiled. "He [smiled. /¶ "He H, N, P
129.21 voice [voice, H, N, P
132.2-4 know." [know. I used to laugh sometimes." - but there was no laughter in his eyes - "to think that you didn't know." H, N, P
132.6 ago [ago, H, N, P
132.15 more [more, H, N, P

137.2 *no break* [*break* H, N, P
140.10 "M-a-y ["M-a-v H, N, P
153.7 left, [left N, P
154.1 to-day [today N, P
160.24 *no break* [*break* N, P
167.26 *no break* [*break* N, P
172.13 said [sid N, P
173.19 that, [that N, P
175.3-5 it?" /¶ "Jimmy [it?" /¶ "It just shows you." /¶ "Jimmy N, P
175.19 *no break* [*break* N, P
179.21 *no break* [*break* N, P
181.7 *no break* [*break* N, P

III

Tender is the Night: Variants between the First (A-1.60) and Latest (L-2.67) Printings of the Scribner Library Edition

KEY

The first reading is that of the first printing (A-1.60), the second that of the latest printing (L-2.67).

49.6 rabit [rabbit
69.6 up now. [now."
69.1 up sot [not
167.3 might [mighty
261.7 up person- [person
311.6 up righ [high
32.4 up eveyone [everyone
68.19 Gerogian [Georgian
82.10 up Not [No
118.5 looling [lolling
120.7 Kreuzegg [Krenzegg
122.26 was [has
168.20 Gausses [Gausse's
314.17 "As [As

Editing Hofmannsthal
Some Remarks
Concerning a New Edition

RICHARD EXNER

In this paper I shall attempt to describe some problems connected with editing Hugo von Hofmannsthal (1874-1929) and, by implication, with the forthcoming critical edition of Hofmannsthal's collected works, which the Freies Deutsches Hochstift in Frankfurt/Main is undertaking. My task is made difficult because there are some fundamental reflections which I should like to outline. Another difficulty arises from the present stage of the edition, perhaps best described as a pre-prolegomena stage. The editors are at the time of writing (late 1969) still formulating editorial principles, and some of these remarks are therefore rather tentative. But there is an advantage in that I have an opportunity to indicate some options and alternatives before they have been officially ruled out. My own position, and this should be understood from the outset, is not that of a chief editor, of whom there will be five. I am one of what will probably be a sizable team of co-editors, each of whom will edit one or several, or perhaps parts of several, volumes. Finally, the various problems I shall try to enumerate are interrelated, and thus the difficulties are compounded. Specific examples toward the end of my paper will perhaps best illustrate why the risks and stakes

I am greatly indebted to the Simon J. Guggenheim Memorial Foundation for making it possible for me to examine substantial areas of Hofmannsthal's Nachlass.

in a new edition of Hofmannsthal's works seem to me to be particularly high.

It would be satisfying if the paper could focus its attention on the technical aspects of the new edition only, but this is impossible. Decisions concerning these technical aspects will, in part, be dictated by more general reflections. A formidable task lies ahead, and with some slight exaggeration one might sum up all the problems and difficulties by saying that if ever there was a critical edition of a modern writer which seems doomed, in some respects at least, to partial failure, not only today but probably always, it is any edition of Hugo von Hofmannsthal's works.

I

The first part of my remarks will be concerned with what I shall call technical problems: questions of size, completeness, inclusiveness, and structure of the edition as well as questions arising from the relatively large size of its editorial staff. The second part will treat inherent difficulties and will therefore focus on Hofmannsthal's method of composition.

The first edition of Hofmannsthal's collected works, prepared under the poet's direction, was published in six small volumes by S. Fischer in 1924.[1] Five years after his death, in 1934, a second edition, somewhat enlarged, was published in three substantial volumes, also by S. Fischer.[2] During the next dozen years, mostly under the guidance of Hofmannsthal's son-in-law, Professor Heinrich Zimmer, who had complete editorial discretion, various texts and letters from the Nachlass were published in the Swiss journal *Corona.*[3] After World War II the edition that is still on the market today was begun. Herbert Steiner, the editor of *Corona*, also edited this fifteen-volume Hofmannsthal edition, *Gesammelte Werke in Einzelausgaben* (1945ff.)[4] Steiner

1 / Hugo von Hofmannsthal, *Gesammelte Werke* (Berlin: S. Fischer, 1924) six volumes

2 / Hugo von Hofmannsthal, *Gesammelte Werke* (Berlin: S. Fischer, 1934) three volumes

3 / *Corona* (Zweimonatsschrift), herausgegeben von Martin Bodmer und Herbert Steiner, 1930ff

publised in 1959 an account of his edition, *Bericht und Berichtigung,*[5] partially in response to a detailed and severe criticism of it by Werner Volke.[6] At this time the British Hofmannsthal scholar Michael Hamburger voiced some basic considerations, which I should like to indicate below.[7] They are all the more important today when the present edition is embarking on what appears to be a huge venture with possibly as many as 2½ dozen or more individual editors.

Writers such as Hofmannsthal, Rilke, George, Benn, Trakl, Kafka, Thomas Mann, Musil, and Broch have, in terms of history, died only recently. Yet their works are thought to be "classical" and well worth not only the enormous scholarly effort of commentary and analysis expended on them since their authors' death or, in some cases, even during their lifetime, but also the necessary philological effort to reissue them in critical editions. With the exception of Trakl, none of these writers has, to date, been canonized or ossified in an "historical-critical" edition. The reason is, of course, physical, that is, chronological impossibilities: many of their papers are still sealed, are in private hands, or are otherwise unobtainable. One might, however, wonder whether in the light of recent developments in scholarship and of the technical perfection of manuscript reproduction such complete editions will be desirable in the future.

Quite often some other solution than a full edition is found: the desirable and the possible are fused in a kind of sophisticated "complete" or "collected" works with a re-

4 / Hugo von Hofmannsthal, *Gesammelte Werke in Einzelausgaben,* herausgegeben von Herbert Steiner (Stockholm: Bermann-Fischer and Frankfurt/Main: S. Fischer, 1945ff.), fifteen volumes. The only other edition in print is one edited by Rudolf Hirsch: *Ausgewählte Werke in zwei Bänden* (Frankfurt/Main: S. Fischer, 1957, 1961)

5 / Herbert Steiner, *Zur Hofmannsthal-Ausgabe,* I: *Bericht und Berichtigung* (Bern: Paul Haupt, 1959)

6 / Werner Volke, 'Die neue Ausgabe der Werke Hugo von Hofmannsthals,' *Deutsche Vierteljahrsschrift für Literaturwissenschaft und Geistesgeschichte* 32 (1958) 305-15

7 / Michael Hamburger, review of H. Steiner's report on his edition (see note 5) in *German Life and Letters* 14 (1960/61) 101f. Later in my paper I refer to Hamburger's 'Hofmannsthals Bibliothek,' *Euphorion* 55 (1961) 15-76.

spectable but not exhaustive scholarly apparatus. Nevertheless, to use Mr Hamburger's words, the question is 'vexed and controversial', especially in Germany. Although every one at first seems willing to settle for some kind of edition which will at least supply reliable texts, scholars are quick to carp and censure when it appears. Arrangement, completeness, and apparatus are always questioned. Mr Hamburger reminds us that English writers of comparable status 'rarely attain the dignity of a collected edition so soon after their death.' From this point of view, the interim solution in the case of W.B. Yeats must seem ideal, yet it might be recalled that the Prag-Reichenberg edition of Stifter was begun less than forty years after Stifter's death. And Hofmannsthal died in 1929.

There are of course practical considerations in determining the scope of an edition. The more detailed and complete the edition is, the more cumbersome it often becomes for lay readers, and by lay readers I mean those who are trained to read scholarly texts if need be but who also simply wish to have a readable yet reliable edition. This consideration prompted the format of the Steiner edition: a collected works, printed in fifteen volumes purchasable separately, each of them reprintable if the need should arise. Many of the individual volumes of this edition have gone through several printings, in some cases with a slight change of format (not affecting the external appearance), with corrections, and more than once, *horribile dictu*, with new pagination. The harsh review by Dr Volke was published in 1958, when fourteen of these fifteen volumes had appeared. It stated flatly: 'A critical edition is as yet impossible.'

We must ask, almost a dozen years later: is it possible today? And even ask - under our breath - will it be possible a dozen years hence? Professor Martin Stern's scholarly edition of *Silvia im Stern* has a critical apparatus of almost one hundred closely printed pages following the text of the comedy; quite rightly, I think, the disclaimer is added that this is not an "historical-critical" edition, and that there can never be such an edition of one single work by itself. Contemplating this complexity, one might well ask to what end and into what straits perfectionism, nineteenth-century tradition, and the striving for an ideal edition have led.

But back to earth. Reality commands that this edition of Hofmannsthal must be prepared while eminently devoted and qualified men are alive, while invaluable sources of information are available, while there seems to be a publisher who, with some subvention, is willing to embark upon a basically unpredictable enterprise, and while, finally, general interest in Hofmannsthal is quite high. The question, in other words, is the limits of a *possible* edition which will not be superseded for many years.

It is regrettable in this connection that an extraordinarily rich and varied Nachlass has not been given interim publication. Preparation and publication of four volumes of Nachlass texts had been outlined by Herbert Steiner and were still actively contemplated in 1961,[8] but his plan was never realized. It was delayed by Dr Steiner's illness and abandoned after his death. These four volumes would by now have fully acquainted the scholarly and general audience with several works of Hofmannsthal's which, under present circumstances, may not be published for years. They would thus have rounded out and, in a preliminary fashion, determined a total view of the poet and would have made it possible to delay, in good conscience, the present plans until an even more suitable basis for the edition could have been established.

There is, then, no doubt that the edition now in the planning stage will have to compromise somewhat between the requirements of scholarly research and wider popularity. Thus the publisher is said to have reserved the right to print, separately, individual texts hitherto unpublished, thereby reducing the potential audience of the large edition.

And there is still another elementary and sobering consideration. For many years, before the advent of copyright-devouring xerography, an "historical-critical" edition was,

8 / Herbert Steiner, 'Zur Hofmannsthal-Ausgabe,' in *In Libro Humanitas: Festschrift für Wilhelm Hoffmann* (Stuttgart: Ernst Klett, 1962) 347f

for almost all scholars, virtually the only access to the texts of a writer. One might well ask today, as I mentioned earlier: is an "historical-critical" edition truly necessary? (I hasten to add that the chief editors have taken pains to point out that their goal is not such an edition. They have done so, I believe, not because they think that a super-edition will be forthcoming a few decades hence, but to lower expectations and to impede otherwise unavoidable criticism in advance.) Scholars who must know the exact version of a text can easily obtain a Xerox copy and others could certainly make do with a competently edited text such as, for example, Ernst Zinn has provided in the recently completed Rilke edition. Why, then, invent a plethora of elaborate keys, if by photoelectricity the text can be reproduced perfectly, with a - quite often - clearer 'original' than the manuscript itself. Moreover, the editorial apparatus could become so complicated that a Xerox copy of the original manuscript would present an easier task to the reader. One might indeed argue for an *editio minor* which would concentrate on carefully established texts and which could be enlarged by supplementary volumes, centring around the genesis, structure, and development of major works or of particular clusters of works that occupied Hofmannsthal over a period of many years. Such *pars pro toto* "models" would acquaint lay readers and philologists with Hofmannsthal's creative method. If several of these supplementary volumes could be conceived and executed painstakingly with the help of all of the poet's known sources, they would not only, implicitly, serve as examples for other works but would also make it unnecessary to employ the same editorial effort and detail for each individual piece of Hofmannsthal's writings. An *editio minor* approximating this plan would probably save years. It would also substantially reduce the task of several of the editors, and it would certainly constitute a most appropriate approach to the poet.

For the editors of Hofmannsthal, the task is made both difficult and rewarding by the size of his Nachlass. It contains approximately 33,000 sheets (some of them very small in size) and 8,500 letters, the letters about evenly divided between those written by and those addressed to Hofmannsthal. It is a safe prediction that the major part of these papers, once published, will change the current view of Hofmannsthal (one is tempted to say: whatever this view might now be). The further quandary in which the editors find themselves, however, is that despite its richness the Nachlass is not complete, and at present it seems particularly unfortunate that some folders of material are for various reasons as yet unavailable for study and evaluation. There is, for instance, the folder containing material for *Die Frau ohne Schatten*. There are the papers connected with Hofmannsthal's literary and personal relationship with Stefan George. Both manuscript groups are in private hands. In a third example - the important correspondence between Hofmannsthal and Lily Geyger-Schalk - there is an objective time problem. Other groups of correspondence are still unexamined and unpublished in their entirety (such as the complete correspondence with Hermann Bahr, Rudolf Pannwitz, and Rudolf Alexander Schröder, and the letters to Countess Ottonie Degenfeld), but it is clear that the Schalk correspondence especially would aid not only in settling problems in the dating of some of the early poems but also in questions of interpretation. These letters are now deposited in the National Library of Vienna and will remain sealed until the year 2007. Also, a good many letters Hofmannsthal wrote to his parents, to his wife, and to his children will remain unavailable for publication for the time being. These hindrances need not delay - and I am not suggesting they should - the new edition. The accuracy and completeness of components of this edition will necessarily vary, however. This is cause for regret only in the light of the chances of an edition superseding ours.

Another source of information - and I see no reason why it should not be included under the general heading of Nachlass - is what is left of Hofmannsthal's library, approximately 2,400 volumes. This figure does not include some 800 items belonging directly, together with the correspondence, to the Nachlass and consisting predominantly of desk copies of his own works, his private collection of offprints of his works that appeared in journals and newspapers (frequently with handwritten comments and corrections), works to which he had contributed, and works he had edited or introduced, as well as books and offprints about his work. In his youth Hofmannsthal was a voracious reader, throughout his life a creative one. The reading lists which the sixteen and seventeen-year-old poet had not only drawn up for himself but also absorbed are truly stunning. Some years ago, in an acclaimed article in *Euphorion*, Michael Hamburger drew attention to the extent of Hofmannsthal's reading and to the method. His method did not consist (as in the case of Thomas Mann) merely of copious marking and underlining, but included actual composition during or after the reading: on the end-papers of books there are important notes and parts of scenes, early stages of scenarios perhaps eventually discarded, etc. That this collection of books and "marginal" writings can be of considerable importance is shown, to give only one example, by the simple fact that a work which commentators often treat slightingly, *Die ägyptische Helena*, was composed against the sombre background of *Der Turm* (this fact alone should have prevented any slighting); moreover, entries in various books indicate that the work occupied Hofmannsthal far more intensively than any "occasional" piece could have done. In short, these additional sources from the poet's library must also be catalogued and made available to the editors.

What does all this unpublished material have to do with Hofmannsthal's collected or complete works? Surely these bits and pieces are not works if the term is to have any significance at all. This question raises a vexing problem which is faced by many editors and which cannot be fully argued here. It includes the consideration whether a poet's letters are "works." Rilke stated repeatedly that part of his creative productivity went into epistolary efforts; Ernst Zinn, if only because of the enormous quantity of Rilke's letters, did not include them in his recent edition. Hofmannsthal's attitude toward his letters was, I believe, far more equivocal. A dozen or more of his exchanges of correspondence, edited by various hands, with uneven competence, are available and are vigorously exploited by Hofmannsthal scholars. The fact that I raise the problem of para-textual and biographical evidence indicates not only its importance for the edition but also my personal prejudice.

An eminent Canadian Germanist, Professor Barker Fairley, has reminded us that 'Erlebnis and all that'[9] is ultimately of questionable value. He recalls that in the nineteenth century, when some of the great "historical-critical" editions were conceived of and completed, scholars were content to set forth facts in an edition. The only case in which he feels indulgence is indicated is that of Goethe, because poetry to him was incidental to the art and mastery of living. He rightly reminds us that the search for experiences, extra-literary biographical events documented in notes or letters, could and should never become a search for criteria of literary excellence. Such experiences and events may illuminate a work, but they cannot enhance it nor can they improve its quality. Yet, I submit, these events are facts also. If we go but a step farther we must disregard all written attempts made by a poet to write a poem, we must discard (if he did not have the good judgment to do it himself), or at least ignore, the variants and sketches. Such a limitation would, I think, seriously impoverish any view of that particular poet and of the creative act of writing itself. In Hofmannsthal's case an editor cannot ignore (particularly for reasons that will appear a little farther on) certain documented experiences. They will not only aid him in dating a poem, they will also help him decide between this or that version of a poem (if a choice has to be made); they may ultimately not only illuminate the poem but illuminate it to the point of first comprehension; and by making clear the context of the poem they may - is it not possible? - thereby indeed change

9 / Barker Fairley, '*Erlebnis* and all that,' *Seminar* 1 (1965) 1-8

its quality, its relative standing in the entire oeuvre. This is an eternal question, and I shall not attempt a final answer. The truth, as so often in our profession, resides in the nuances of the application of the method. Erlebnis-hunting will not do; nor, however, will hermeneutic and ascetic limitation of one's resources to the text, only the text, and nothing but the text. What is the text, after all, but the configuration of many components, some of them external, some internal, in relation to the poetic nucleus of a poem; in other words, is text not context already?

Hofmannsthal, lest we get lost in mystification, has an apparently much simpler answer. Asked by Ruth Rilke, less than half a year after her famous father's death, what he might wish to contribute to her father's memory by way of personal reminiscences, he wrote rather curtly that if he felt his own end to be near he would 'alles tun - so weit sich in dieser zerfahrenen Welt etwas tun lässt - diese vielen schalen und oft indiscreten Äusserungen über einen productiven Menschen und seine Hervorbringungen, dieses verwässernde Geschwätz, zu unterdrücken, zumindest ihm möglichst die Nahrung zu entziehen durch Bei-Seite bringen der privaten Briefe und Aufzeichnungen, Erschwerung des läppischen Biographismus und aller dieser Unziemlichkeiten.'[10] *Individuum est ineffabile,* Hofmannsthal had repeatedly stated. It is quite possible that this letter should not be taken at face value. Undoubtedly, Hofmannsthal was trying to extricate himself tactfully from a situation that had caused him some embarrassment. Yet the remarks uttered on this occasion are quite valid for Hofmannsthal himself. We should believe him

10 / This letter to Ruth Sieber-Rilke, written on 24 April 1927, was first published in *Corona,* 10 (1943), 800-1. The translation of this and other passages in this paper is my own: '... do everything - as much as can be done in this distracted world - to suppress these many flat and often indiscreet utterances about a creative person and his works, to suppress and diminish this insipid gossip by doing away with private letters and notes, thus making this silly biographism and other similar improprieties a great deal more difficult ... After this struggle is won, a new spiritual entity of the poet will emerge victorious and remain unassailable.' I cite the German text of this letter as it is published (following the manuscript) in *Hofmannsthal Blätter* 2 (1969) 85.

when he asks that this 'ineffable individual' be surrendered to death and oblivion; the works alone should undertake the difficult and secret struggle against the hostile decades of the future, 'aus dem dann, wenn er siegreich bestanden ist, ein neues geisterhaftes Wesen mit solcher Kraft als Sieger hervorgeht und unantastbar dasteht.' Is this statement, under the circumstances and predicaments of a critical edition, to be taken to heart? (One need only think of Franz Kafka's last will as it is related to his creative work, of Max Brod's decision, and his edition of Kafka's works, to become fully aware of the consequences.) After all, Hofmannsthal not only preserved a wealth of biographical material from practically every year of his creative life but did so in the face of frequent presentiments of death in his later years (some of them obvious to us from the letters to C.J. Burckhardt). He also stated repeatedly that his work was full of 'enormously biographical' aspects (I translate 'furchtbar biographisch' in the least negative way).

If the editors concentrate on the works alone they will most certainly arrive at a different image of Hofmannsthal from the one that would emerge from an edition that leaves nothing unpublished. Are they to take into consideration what the poet himself thought of his work? The esteem in which he held individual works changed, and they cannot possibly let this change determine their criteria. But must his views be ignored altogether? And are they, furthermore, to worry whether the Hofmannsthal image their edition creates will ultimately become identical with the 'spiritual entity'? Are they, in other words, entitled to offer what, in the face of Hofmannsthal's intentions, may amount to a falsification in the name of scholarship, an idol at the altar of which taste and tact are so often sacrificed? The question is not rhetorical, nor is it idle or moot. The present plan for the edition calls for at least thirty-six volumes! The predilections and convictions of the chief editors will certainly be decisive. Whatever the degree of caution, I believe they feel that we cannot ignore the vast amount of material besides the works. If a historico-critical view (inspired by such figures as Lukács, Adorno, and Szondi) were to prevail, there would result quite a different edition from one directed by people, on the other extreme, to whom Hofmannsthal's works are a kind of revelation. This hypothesis, though exaggerated, is useful: a large team of editors will certainly be guided by varying editorial philosophies, no matter how strictly any technical editorial principles which are established might be adhered to.

The importance of viable editorial principles, however, cannot be overestimated, precisely because of the different backgrounds and viewpoints of the individual editors. Their philosophies might well be mutually exclusive. The present chief editors have taken great care to establish preliminary principles which, they hope, will be acceptable to all editors. They have decided to rely heavily on the editorial principles that are guiding the Brentano edition, also being prepared under the auspices of Freies Deutsches Hochstift. I believe that Brentano and Hofmannsthal were not only very different authors but that the materials from which both editions work are not completely comparable. Still, it is easy to accept a stipulation that spelling and punctuation in the edition shall always be the poet's, that various versions of any given work shall not be fused to create an optimal composite text, and that lucidity and clarity shall guide the editors in their presentation of the text. It is considerably more difficult to imagine the consequences arising from the distinction the chief editors see between a "historical-critical" and a "critical" edition. The latter, while presenting all texts and (presumably) all variants will not give (even by way of commentary) all of the author's sources, thus sharply reducing the critical apparatus. It seems to me, however, that an editor must nevertheless do most of the work necessary for an "historical-critical" edition if he wishes to present a reliable text and a knowledgeable commentary. In a possible *editio minor*, for example, an editor would spend the same amount of time, no matter whether he chose to present the entire history of a text or simply chose to report, in a commentary, on all data relevant to the chronology, order, and pre-final stages of a text. But he would spend this time on selected works only. The time element cannot be ignored; many of the editors do not live in or near Frankfurt, almost none of them will be editing on a full-time basis, and the major portion of the Nachlass papers are on loan to Freies Deutsches Hochstift for a limited number of years.

The tentative table of contents of the edition foresees two volumes for lyric poetry, twenty-two volumes for the plays, including the comedies, ballets, scenarios, pantomimes, and unfinished sketches, and ten volumes for the prose. The sequence within each section will be generic rather than chronological. In the 'prose' section, the stories will be separated from the essayistic writing and the imaginary letters and conversations. Two volumes of that section are to be given over to autobiographical writing (*Buch der Freunde*, 'Ad me ipsum,' already published) and the large body of notes, some of which were published in volume XV of the Steiner edition (*Aufzeichnungen*), gathered under 'Notizen und Fragmente I and II.' A volume with, I assume, various indices is planned.*

*This tentative table of contents is published *in extenso* and explained by Detlev Lüders, one of the chief editors, in an article (*Jahrbuch für Internationale Germanistik* 1 [1969] 169-78) which also describes the entire Nachlass in much more detail than I have been able to do in this paper.

At a more recent editorial conference at Frankfurt, another classification for the table of contents was advanced which, in essence, has now been adopted. There are to be three series (Reihen). The first will consist of the works authorized by the author and published during his lifetime. To each volume of this series will be added a supplementary volume with relevant variants, a history of publication, a justification of the chosen wording of the texts, etc. The second series will present works not authorized by the author or published only in part. This will include works which remained unpublished because of the poet's death. A third series will concentrate on autobiographical works, on notes, and on fragments. This plan creates several new problems. It tends to separate groups of works that belong together. Although it does not solve the difficult problem of genre for Hofmannsthal, it relies on the poet's own classifications in the 1924 edition. The new table of contents will, by making a definite distinction between finished and unfinished works, also tend to obscure the over-all fragmentary character of Hofmannsthal's oeuvre (see especially Richard Alewyn's remarks later in this paper). [R.E./May 1970]

At an even more recent conference, primarily because of financial pressures and considerations of time, the pro's and con's of an *editio minor* were discussed anew. A compromise in the direction of such an edition seems very likely now. [R.E./December 1970]

The generic categories are logical yet very difficult to apply. Think only of the problems connected with 'Lyrische Dramen', 'Kleine Dramen', 'drame lyrique'! Hofmannsthal did not make any definite distinctions in this realm, one reason being that some of these pieces were written as libretti for Richard Strauss. The 1924 and 1934 editions list *Ariadne* as 'Lyrisches Drama'; Steiner printed it with the comedies (*Lustspiele* III). Hofmannsthal also did not truly distinguish between the various kinds of prose; an accomplished essayist, as he was assured he was by his friends and critics, he abhorred the term "essay" and viewed the whole genre as unacceptable. His prose pieces are only classifiable with the help of artificial categories. Moreover, he frequently treated one theme in several genres and at different times of his life. It could easily happen that he 'finished' a work at a point in time when he apparently had already abandoned the subject years earlier. I believe that in Hofmannsthal's particular case no truly satisfactory alternative arrangement exists. Whether chronology or subject-matter (thematic and topical contexts) should be of primary importance cannot be resolved without compromise. Purely philological requirements would of course militate in favour of chronological order, regardless of contextual preference. This order, however, would ignore the importance of the inner structure of Hofmannsthal's work. Strict chronology, even within sections such as 'lyric poetry,' 'prose,' 'drama,' would separate many intimately connected works - works which might be grouped under such headings as 'Abenteurer,' 'Ödipus,' and 'Turm.' Hofmannsthal himself, in the edition of 1924, disregarded chronology in the interest of a more unifying principle. His decision has proved a constant problem for editors and scholars. In the edition still on the market, to give but one example, Herbert Steiner edited the prose sketch (it is more than that, actually) *Lucidor* in the volume *Erzählungen* (Hofmannsthal himself had issued it as 'Erzählung' in the 1924 edition of his collected works) and the libretto for *Arabella*, written eighteen years later, in *Lustspiele* IV. In the new edition these two works will most likely be treated by two different editors. This is just one example of how chronology and genre will complicate the work of the editors. Even with editorial supererogation, there will be a knotty problem which must result, at the very least, in a system of cross-references.

This point raises the whole spectre of uniformity without monotony, of adequate safeguards to protect Hofmannsthal's texts from levelling editorial techniques and individual editors from centralized policies, yet also of protecting the edition from the editorial and interpretative whims and idiosyncrasies of individual editors, who do not believe in teamwork, who are separated by geographical distances, and who will want to leave their individual mark on their volume. Truly, the task of final editorial scrutiny is awe-inspiring.

II

What I have said so far is, even in some of its technical aspects, largely Zukunftsmusik. I should like to devote the remainder of this paper to the inherent difficulties of editing Hofmannsthal. I also think it is high time to use not only words like 'problem' and 'difficulty,' but also the word 'challenge,' and to speak of the sources of continuing discovery and of the joy and excitement that come with such discovery. It was a discovery of this nature that set me on the path of further exploration into the astonishing wealth of Hofmannsthal's œuvre. Seven years ago I had a first look into what Herbert Steiner described in the *Harvard Library Bulletin* as 'sheets and sheets of single keywords for situations and characters, dialogues, scenarios, and almost finished single acts, difficult to decipher, written as if breathlessly, allusively ...'[11] I became familiar with a method of literary creation which must often have found its fulfilment in the very act of allusion, configuration, of incipient but not executed perfection. Steiner judged inspiration to be of the first importance for Hofmannsthal. This inspiration, he stated,

11 / Herbert Steiner, 'The Harvard Collection of Hugo von Hofmannsthal,' *Harvard Library Bulletin* 8 (1954) 54-64

'was not always matched by an equal power of construction.' The wealth of the Nachlass, the variety of sketches, supports the opinion that Hofmannsthal invented more easily than he formulated. He often cited, probably not in self-defence, unless he did so unwittingly, the sentence: 'Die Gestalt erledigt das Problem' (Form eliminates the problem). Most of the problems he wrote about were continuous for him. What Steiner called the 'power of construction' became, especially during the later years of his life, a precarious thing, dependent on many circumstances, in part beyond the poet's control. We can say this and still value highly the importance and peculiar quality of "unfinishedness" in Hofmannsthal's writings.

Richard Alewyn, the leading German Hofmannsthal scholar, has recently stressed this quality again, developing what almost amounts to a metaphysics from the fragmentary nature of most of the major subjects in Hofmannsthal's writing. His sudden death was but an instance of interruption; his work, says Alewyn, would always have been unfinished: 'it was intended, as it were, for completion in infinity.'[12] What Borchardt, in a letter to C.J. Burckhardt, called 'die Geisterwelt der Entwürfe'[13] (the spirit world of sketches) was the foundation on which his entire oeuvre, both the ostensibly finished part and the large unfinished part, rested. We do well to recognize the strong Platonic current in Hofmannsthal's writing and thinking.

The earlier versions and the sketches are the roots of unlimited possibilities, according to Alewyn, who also extends the concept of "pre-existence" into the work itself, interpreting as "pre-existent" work that remained unfinished. Yet Hofmannsthal never really abandoned a subject. Nearly all the themes he had ever touched upon he saw as related and relatable within a network of configuration he alone

12 / Professor Alewyn's lecture 'Hofmannsthals unvollendetes Werk,' which was delivered as the principal address at the first meeting of the Hofmannsthal society in September 1968, has not yet been published. It was summarized by L.M. Fiedler in *Hofmannsthal Blätter* 2 (1969) 142f.

13 / Cited in Rudolf Hirsch's report on 'Die Handschriften im Besitz der Familie Hofmannsthal' in *Hofmannsthal Blätter* 2 (1969) 8

could master, an intricate almost three-dimensional chess game where every move, even the slightest, was of consequence to each figure on the board. Thus he never finished an epoch of his life, crowning it with some particularly significant work, as did, for example, both Goethe and Rilke. The foremost living connoisseur of Hofmannsthal's life and work, Dr Rudolf Hirsch, who has for years inspired inquiry and research, has recently shown (and the findings are documented by the poet's notes, found in desk copies of his own works) that Hofmannsthal returned to the Sobeide theme of 1897 again in 1908, to *Der Kaiser und die Hexe* (1897) in 1919, to the Oedipus material (1903ff.) in 1923, and to *Cristinas Heimreise* (1907ff.) as late as 1926, in other words, years after these works had ostensibly been 'completed.'[14] We also know from his correspondence that a feeling of the insufficiency of the "finished" works often befell him and that once again he would take up the same topic on a different level of his creative imagination. Late in 1926, in answer to a request for permission to use *Der Kaiser und die Hexe* for a performance, Hofmannsthal wrote quite unforgettably about a 'secret but decisive shortcoming' of his early play: 'Dass Sie gerade dieses Spiel wählen, berührt mich eigen. Dass ich es verfasst habe, liegt lange zurück, volle 29 Jahre. Trotzdem ist mir dieses Gedicht nicht ferne gerückt, ja gewissermassen hat es sich noch gar nicht völlig von mir gelöst. Ich denke oft daran, nicht so, wie man an eine abgeschlossene Arbeit denkt, *sondern eher wie an einen Plan oder Entwurf*.'[15] This passage seems to furnish ample proof for the view that Hofmannsthal never fully abandoned a subject (in this particular instance, the central topic was important during the many years in which he wrote *Die Frau ohne Schat-*

14 / Cf. ibid., 80f.

15 / Italics mine. 'It gives me a strange feeling that you have chosen this particular play. It has been twenty-nine years since I wrote it. Yet it never moved away from me; it has not even now detached itself from me. I often think of it, but not as one thinks of a completed work, rather as if it were still a plan, a sketch.' This letter to Georg Terramare was published in Wolfgang Nehring, *Die Tat bei Hofmannsthal* (Stuttgart: J. B. Metzlersche Verlagsbuchhandlung, 1966) 142f.

ten) and also that, fundamentally, he could not conceive of a final irrevocable version of his plays. In the same letter he tries to explain this habit further. 'Ich glaube zu verstehen, woher dies kommt: daher, dass ich als recht junger Mensch in dieser Arbeit einen sehr grossen, wahrhaft tiefen Stoff ergriffen habe, aber in halb traumwandelnder Weise, ohne ihm ganz gewachsen zu sein.'[16]

Hofmannsthal's working habits are, of course, also revealed in the "notes." One sheet, sometimes folded over several times, shows entries referring and belonging to several works all at once. Here is an additional but not insuperable difficulty for the edition: besides the necessary identification of unidentified entries, all entries have to be separated and added to the relevant individual text folders. The same procedure must be followed for entries in the letters. This will eventually assure each editor that the folders which contain his text also contain *all* references to it from the correspondence and all other parts of the Nachlass. Hofmannsthal's mind did not work systematically, not in a chronologically observable manner. Take, for example, the month of May 1917 (and any number of instances could be given, even more readily from earlier years such as 1897).[17] I should like to cite two passages from letters. The first was to Rudolf Borchardt. Hofmannsthal speaks of having been almost in a fever of inner motion during that month: '... ich concipierte oder hallucinierte zwölf oder zwanzig oder dreissig Stücke einer Prosa neuer Form ...'[18] And to Hermann Bahr: 'Ich war im Mai fast nicht imstande, das auf mich eindringende von Gedanken - oder wie nenne ich es besser: Aufforderungen, Ahnungen, Verbindungen, zu bewältigen. Es rührt dann ein

16 / 'I think I understand why this is so: As a rather young man I had taken up a very great and truly deep subject in this play, but in a half somnambulant way without being quite ready for it.'

17 / During late August and early September of 1897, at Varese, Hofmannsthal worked on and, for the most part, completed *Das kleine Welttheater, Die Frau im Fenster, Der weisse Fächer, Die Hochzeit der Sobeide,* and *Der Kaiser und die Hexe.*

18 / Hugo von Hofmannsthal/Rudolf Borchardt, *Briefwechsel* (Frankfurt/Main: S. Fischer, 1954) 127. The letter was written on 7 July 1917: '... I conceived of or hallucinated twelve or twenty or thirty items in a new kind of prose ...'

Windhauch hundert gespannte Saiten an, hunderterlei ist bei mir angefangen, angelegt, ist innere Möglichkeit, Plan, untermalte Leinwand, antizipiertes Gedicht, noch nicht gereiftes aperçu, alles greift doch ineinander, Gedicht, politische Ahnung, Roman, Comödie, Aphorisma, Briefe, Relationen. Es ist ungeheuer schwer, alles zusammen und alles auseinander zu halten ... ich arbeite, wenn ich bei mir selbst bin, mit einer Präsenz des Vielfältigen, die ich kaum erklären kann."[19] This type of creative method is difficult to illustrate in an edition that is to remain readable, except by facsimile reproduction of manuscript pages. Caution must also be exercised lest a reader gain the impression that Hofmannsthal's writing depended entirely on such times as the fall of 1897 or May of 1917. Herbert Steiner pointed out that no matter how hastily some of the impressions seem to have been set down, his work also advanced with a noticeable steadiness. And Rudolf Hirsch reminds us (although it is probably hard for some of us to imagine that Hofmannsthal would not make notes on what is most important): 'the poet makes frequent notations when he distrusts his memory. Things, however, that his imagination is absolutely sure of and that he *cannot* lose, he does not jot down.'[20]

Figure 1 shows two manuscript pages from his earlier years: one contains the variants and part of the final version of the poem 'Lebenslied,' dated 23 February 1896, the other, variants of its second strophe. This is a poem for which there is a fair copy of a four- and a five-strophe version. The new edition must show or reproduce the variants because, I believe, it is only with the help of these variants

19 / The letter to Bahr, written on 17 August 1917, was first published in *Die Neue Rundschau* 59 (1948) 221f.: 'During May I was almost incapable of coping with the onrush of thoughts, or I had better say challenges, presentiments, interconnections. One breath of wind touches upon a hundred taut strings, hundreds of things in me are then begun, conceived, become inner possibility, plan, readied canvas, anticipated poem, an aperçu not yet final; everything is interrelated, poem, political presentiment, novel, comedy, aphorism, letters, relationships. It is incredibly difficult to keep things together and keep them apart ... When I am quite myself, I can work in the presence of an almost inexplicable variety.'

20 / Rudolf Hirsch, *Hofmannsthal Blätter* 2 (1969) 80

[illegible]

Das Fellboot aus den Händen
der todten alten Frau
[illegible]
Das lächelnd sie verschwinden
An Adler, Lamm und Pfau

Die Todten die entgleiten
Die Schiffel in den weiten
[illegible] sind sie nicht das Schönste
der Jünglinge [illegible]

Ein Schwarm von wilden Bienen
Nimmt seine Seele fest.
Das Auge von Delphinen
[illegible] Umgibt
[illegible] mit Gewalt

[illegible] hatte alle Leiden
[illegible]
Mit dunkelblinden Geberden
[illegible] Klein [illegible]
[illegible]
[illegible]
Er ist ein junger Hirt
Den ganzen Mittag
Umarmt er den Mittag

Er löst seine Finger
Und gießt sich wieder hin

Die Schattenlosen Frauen
Des Meeres und der Luft
Sind auf- und [illegible]
In tausendfachen Gruft
[illegible]
Erkennet er Gefühlten
Und schreibt in den Gärten
[illegible] den [illegible]
Des seligen Verwehten
Des Lebens auf und ab
Und schaut den Abgrund
Die [illegible] unbewohnten
Abgründe und die Höhen
Des Leben Tage [illegible]

–

Wie Lächeln kann es werden
An Adler Lamm und Pfau

[illegible]

Vom Schweifenden [illegible] Er hat [illegible] Seele
[illegible] und behütet Der Toten [illegible] entfernt
Ihm [illegible] an alle Spalten Und [illegible]
Das Leben und der Tod

~~[illegible]~~
[illegible] die Helle
[illegible] die Helle
Er giebt sich jeder Stelle [illegible]
Der [illegible] hin

Umgeben und geleitet
[illegible]
Von [illegible]
[illegible] Tod

1 This manuscript page is reproduced from my book *Hugo von Hofmannsthals 'Lebenslied': Eine Studie* (Heidelberg: Carl Winter Universitätsverlag (1964) with the kind permission of the publisher.

that a particularly obscure line in the fourth strophe can be interpreted. This line 'Er lächelt der Gefährten - ' in turn referred to a fifth strophe (originally placed between what are now the third and fourth strophes of the final printed version) which was later dropped. Rather than evaluating the variants in the critical apparatus, the new edition will print those among them the editors consider relevant to the final text. This must be so even if justifiable questions remain concerning the nature of the 'final text' for an author who, unlike, for example, the poet Gottfried Benn, did not know when a text was truly finished. It is necessary to point out also that Hofmannsthal was a notoriously careless proofreader. The negative consequences of this fact are mitigated by the many available bibliophile editions of individual works. One is certainly justified in assuming that, in most instances, the texts for these editions were prepared with exceptional care. Still, words in the variants for the poetry will remain doubtful, some forever illegible. We do not possess galleys of any of the various editions of the poetry and lyrical dramas. If a discrepancy remains between printed text and manuscript, it might have been caused by a change made by Hofmannsthal during galley or page proof corrections. If an editor gives preference to the manuscript text over what has come to be the accepted standard text of a poem he may be adopting a less valid and less reliable (though undoubtedly earlier) text. Consequently, it will be impossible for the editors especially when editing the poetry, to avoid decisions which will thereafter influence the interpretation of a given poem. The chief editors' repeatedly stated principle that every editor will abstain from interpretative comment cannot alter this fact. In that regard, even an "historical-critical" edition cannot apotheosize pure scholarliness; reine Wissenschaftlichkeit is quite an illusion.

Since Hofmannsthal wrote relatively little poetry, the decision to print all variants would not greatly increase the number of pages. By "all variants" I mean all meaningful variants, disallowing those resulting from misspellings, corrupt and unauthorized printings in newspapers, etc. Yet, one [illegible] Selbstverleidung [illegible] Zustandes, Bringen an Leben [illegible]

Disposition. (B - 2te Teil) [illegible]

Die Anarchie, begriffen: ein gegebenes. Kein Bezug der Natur [illegible] Keine Sprache. [illegible] durch die Epoche

Die Anarchie, überblickt: Führerschaft. [illegible] Zeit.

Georg (George) Rang: Buber Lehrer [illegible] Wassermann [illegible] (viele Mystiker [illegible] nebeneinander)

Lehre / Lehrer [illegible] Große Ausbleibung des Sprechens [illegible]

Eine Sprache: Bedrohung. Neuer Ton, Schrift, Predigt, Sendschreiben. Geheimnis.

Bringen an neue Sprache [illegible]

Neue Formen: neues Drama / neuer Roman

Sinn der Anarchie: durch [illegible] des Stoffes. [illegible]

Konservative Revolution.

Zu überwinden.

Der Geist [illegible]

Neue Polaritäten: überwundene Polarität: Leib Seele - überwundene Polarität:

[illegible] überwundene Polarität: oben - unten [illegible]

[illegible] Katholisch - evangelisch.

[illegible] / neue: Ordnung gegen Ordnungen [illegible]

Einheit muss gesucht werden: aber nicht auf der Fläche des Daseins.

[illegible] Nicht in der Topie sondern in der U-Topie. nicht in dem ὄν - das οὐκ ὄν [illegible]

Reichs-idee. (Italiener [illegible]

[illegible] Staat) Geistiger Raum ist identisch mit politischem Raum.

[illegible] Verengung des Raumes seit dem XVII. Jhd. Partielle Erweiterung mit 1789; Eindringen des [illegible]

Ziel: [illegible]

Ablehnung: [illegible]

Ablehnung: [illegible]

[illegible] die Romantik, Jean Paul

Hölderlin) [illegible]

Die Generation der Überlieferung ergreift sich [illegible]

[illegible] die [illegible]

Verengung des Raumes, Ausschluss von Österreich [illegible] Idee des Staats [illegible]

Österreich: [illegible] Staatsgebilde, nicht werdender Staat. [illegible]

[illegible]

2 I am deeply indebted to Dr Rudolf Hirsch, Frankfurt/Main, for the permission to reproduce this hitherto unpublished manuscript page.

might well question the word "meaningful" further and point out that the nature of extant variants of poems varies greatly among poets. Emil Staiger's essay on C.F. Meyer's poem 'Vor der Ernte' showed that the changes between the many stages of the poem are almost more illuminating than the final text. While some of the variants in Hofmannsthal aid in our comprehension of a poetic text (in Trakl or Hölderlin one is often at a complete loss without the variants), others are of a much more conventional nature, that is, they attempt to reformulate, substitute, rearrange syntax or vocabulary to accommodate rhyme or rhythm. Therefore a judicious selection among the variants seems appropriate. But how can this be accomplished if the editor is to refrain from all (I presume even implicit) critical and interpretative comment? There are difficult decisions ahead for the editors of the poetry. It is even more vexing to have to admit - as I believe we have to - that, fundamentally, Hofmannsthal's method always remains the same, whether he writes poetry or not. And this fact is what really dooms our editorial efforts to a large extent. A page from the early stages of the late essay *Das Schrifttum als geistiger Raum der Nation* (1926/7) is surely convincing (figure 2). On this page he does not distinguish between quotations from his supplementary reading and his own ideas and inspiration. He composes especially the more ambitious essays - and this was one of his most ambitious ones - as a poet, varying his method little if at all.

Such a method naturally became more cumbersome toward the end of his life, quite apart from the type of essay he was attempting in the one being discussed here. By not "finishing" any epoch of his life but rather transforming or metamorphosing it without ever losing the vision of fundamental ideas and dreams, he steadily increased his "materials" - his store of figures, symbols, and configurations. The more he knew, the greater the amount of material absorbed into an essay, the denser the web of configuration - the more arduous was the final act of composition: the abstraction, abbreviation, and distillation. The new edition cannot identify the various chronological and thematic layers of which a page such as the one illustrated is composed but it must, if at all possible, present the text of an essay like this in such a way that scholarly inquirers will not simply have the rather banal question answered: where is it all from? The edition must rather enable scholarship to come to grips with the much more worthwhile investigation: how was all this composed? If we compare this page, or any of the many to follow until a "fair copy" was possible, with the manuscript pages of, say, 'Sebastian Melmoth,' an essay on Oscar Wilde written in 1905, where a subject whose external aspects were infinitely less demanding was treated rather rapidly, we not only understand the agony Hofmannsthal went through before he could deliver the 'Schrifttum' essay as an address at the university of Munich (in a letter to Haas he calls it 'eine monströse Arbeit'[21]) but the almost mystical significance he ascribed to the moment of crystallization when everything suddenly and finally fell into place. No modern edition, not even one as extensive as the present undertaking, can afford to reproduce this type of preparatory composition except by an occasional facsimile. The nearest thing to a complete reproduction is the new "historical-critical" edition of Conrad Ferdinand Meyer by Zeller and Zäch. It prints everything, reproduces - with a battery of sigla and keys - the manuscripts in type, gives invaluable help to the interpreter, and seems to have all materials available. This edition is being printed with the financial support of the municipality of Kilchberg, the city of Zürich, the canton of Zürich and, finally, a research grant from the Swiss federal government. I list this impressive subvention because, short of support of this magnitude - and the Hofmannsthal edition, despite generous grants from Fritz Thyssen Foundation and Deutsche Forschungsgemeinschaft, cannot count on such munificence - a similar venture remains illusory.

21 / Hugo von Hofmannsthal/Willy Haas, *Ein Briefwechsel* (Berlin: Propyläen Verlag, 1968). The letter, referring to the essay-address as 'a monstrous piece of work,' was written on 19 December, and is printed on pp. 71f.

A report such as this cannot be definitive. It can outline, and I hope it has done so, what awaits the editors and readers of the new Hofmannsthal edition. We cannot, and indeed we should not, create an edition that reflects our literary, historical, or political prejudices. Yet every act of critical selection and, by implication, of interpretation, if only the decision which variant to print and which to omit, will undoubtedly betray some of these prejudices. We must, as editors, work with as much self-denial as possible and hope that our efforts will preserve the unique and manifold facets of this writer, will not obscure but illuminate his complex heritage, his sources, the method of his writing, and the nature of his inspiration. Finally, the edition should render all necessary help to his works as they continue what Hofmannsthal called in the letter to Rilke's daughter the struggle with the hostile decades. I can think of no reason why this part of the task should not inspire us.

Editing a Manuscript Virginia Woolf's *The Waves*

JOHN W. GRAHAM

There may be more enterprise in walking naked, but I frankly envy the other contributors to this conference, who have worn with authority and distinction the hallowed vestments stitched so patiently by generations of editors labouring at their sedentary trade in order to give us accurate editions of the texts we all study. In literary studies, the text is king; and the editor of a text dons his editorial garb in order to amplify and certify the glory of the king. But the manuscript of a text is, in effect, a discarded draft, a scarred and dropsical relation of the king - perhaps, indeed, too close a blood relation for comfort - and is best left alone in the rustical retreat of a bottom drawer. For generations, scholars have succeeded in getting into print documents related much more tenuously to the text than is the mass of words out of which the text emerged: letters, diaries, table talk, anecdotes, obiter dicta of all kinds abound, but only in recent years has there begun a serious effort to publish the draft material of literary texts. The economic barrier may explain the scarcity of such material for long narratives; but it cannot explain a similar scarcity for lyric poems. A better explanation, at least in the last hundred years or so, may have been the post-romantic feeling that the draft of a text is more sacredly private than are the sexual peccadilloes, financial disasters, or mystical experiences of the writer in question: the ashes left behind by the Promethean flame should be exposed to public gaze only on brief ritual occasions, preferably in glass cases in the lobby of the British Museum; and they may occasionally be examined by one of priests, who can then allude cryptically in his footnotes to their presumed significance.

Whatever the reason for scholarly indifference to this form of enterprise, it means that we do not have a well-defined body of principles and procedures particularly designed for the editing of draft material, any more than we have a well-designed and complete set of critical instruments for assessing its literary significance. In a paradoxical way, this fact was the strongest incentive I felt to attempt the job, for it aroused the primal itch, the urge to get it all *out*, where every possible student can study it in every possible way. The draft material for a text is, after all, an historical document, like a letter or diary, and should take its place with these other documents in the library stacks. (The first problem of anyone who contemplates editing this sort of work is the compulsion he feels to say what I have just said, to say it not too defensively, and to go on saying it through months of hard labour which many people regard as a complete waste of time and energy.)

But having decided to cope with this psychological hazard as best I could, I confronted a problem peculiarly acute for the editor of the manuscript of a long narrative - the brute size of the thing. The extant manuscript of *The Waves* consists of two complete holograph drafts, written in seven books of blank paper bound for Virginia Woolf by the Hogarth Press, plus a small loose-leaf notebook containing plans, notes, and fragments pertaining to the second draft. The first draft is 399 pages long, the second 347 pages, and the notebook 23 - a total of 769 pages.

The rest of the manuscript has vanished. We know that, in writing the first draft of *The Waves*, Virginia Woolf followed her usual practice of typing up in the afternoon the draft she had written longhand in the morning. According to Leonard

Woolf, this typescript rarely involved extensive revision - it was simply a working version of the holograph, from which she would proceed to real revision. But she was so dissatisfied with the first draft that she decided to rewrite the whole book in longhand. It is clear that she continued, in the second draft, to type up her holograph each day, and that, having completed the second draft, she typed out the entire book, revising extensively as she did so, and reworking some sections at least twice. When she finally had a fair typescript copy, she gave it to her husband to read. The next opportunity to revise came with the proofs, but she seems to have made few revisions, since it took her only one week to read them, a week in which she was also at work on a new book.

All the typescript versions of *The Waves* have been lost or destroyed. According to her husband, Virginia Woolf habitually destroyed these typescript drafts with each of her novels, choosing to keep only the holograph versions. The printer's copy and proofs may well have been lost or destroyed during the war; they have, in any case, disappeared.

Clearly, before setting eyes on a single photoprint, I would have to establish my fundamental principles, work out my procedures, and devise a sequence of procedures to which I would adhere rigidly; for, once I had begun, second thoughts and improvisations would be fatal. In the eighteen months it took to complete various labyrinthine negotiations, I was able to decide what kind of edition I wished to make and how I would have to do it.

Almost all my editorial policies and practices have been governed by one simple proposition: the manuscript of a text is first of all an historical document, and, if it is to be published, preservation of its integrity must govern its editor at all times. An absolutely accurate transcription is his primal obligation, both to the reader and to the manuscript. His second obligation is to keep the text of his transcription as clean and uncluttered as possible, which involves resisting the temptation to supply so many editorial aids that the document is buried beneath their proliferating expertise. His third obligation is to deny himself the indulgence of emendations, of coy assurances (such as that editorial escape hatch, the word *sic*) that some solecism is the author's and not his own, and of footnotes which present his own interpretations or speculations as if they were facts. His job is to give the reader the document as it is, not to tell him what it means. Accuracy, clarity, and simplicity should be his obsessions, and his fatal errors should be sins of omission rather than commission. For a sin of omission can easily be remedied by someone purer than he; but a sin of commission will remain to mar the document until, and if, it is reedited, which is an unlikely possibility.

These principles helped me to solve quite rapidly the first major problem I faced - how to present the two drafts to the reader. At this point I should explain two terms I shall use. The word 'episode' refers to each of the nine major narrative divisions of the text, the portions delivered by the six characters; and the term 'interlude' refers to the descriptive passages which, in the text, are printed in italics.

As far as I could see, there were only two possible ways in which to present the two drafts to the reader. The first was to present them as parallel texts. However gratefully I slipped into this hallowed vestment, I soon realized that it would not fit. Virginia Woolf habitually revised by rewriting whole sentences, paragraphs, speeches, and sometimes whole episodes. To take a tiny example, Louis' speech as he stands alone in the garden in the first episode, a speech taking a little over a page in the text, has four versions in the first draft and one in the second, for a total of eight pages. Each version differs extensively from the others. How 'parallel' could these be made? Worse still, the entire episode in which the speech occurs is completely rewritten twice in the first draft. An attempt to present as parallel texts the five manuscript versions of this speech and the three versions of this episode would force me to butcher the original document beyond recognition, and to create machinery for editorial guidance which would be so complicated as to be unusable.

The other possible method was the only one that could be followed: to present the two drafts sequentially, in the order in which they were written. This method would satisfy my basic desire to respect the integrity of the document itself, and it would be easy to follow, for the sequence of composition is virtually beyond doubt, simply because Virginia Woolf wrote in bound books of blank paper. Fidelity to the sequence of composition would also preserve for study the complete context of each version of Louis' speech, and would leave entirely visible all traces of the larger strategies which Virginia Woolf followed in her prolonged struggle with certain problems. It would throw into relief, for example, the literary problem of narrative point of view in the text by revealing that Virginia Woolf struggled to retain a first-person omniscient narrator throughout the first draft and on into the second. Or again, it would show how, in the first draft, the interludes are much shorter, more frequent, and more directly integrated into the episodes than they are in the text, where they are sharply separated from each other by spatial and typographical conventions.

My decision to follow this second method of presentation was easy to make, but it produced my next set of problems, all of them involving my obligation to help the reader to collate for himself. The first and most obvious aid would be to produce the transcription in two volumes, so that he could at least place the two drafts side by side for comparison; and this will be done. The second would be to provide in a footnote to a given passage the numbers of every other manuscript page on which he would find versions of the passage, along with the page references for the passage in the standard American and British editions of the text; and this will be done. In a moment of *furor editorialis*, I conceived the most valuable aid of all: to make each of my volumes a looseleaf book, so that the reader could remove all the versions of a specific passage for close comparison and could then restore them to their proper locations in the manuscript. This plan will not be used, partly because a well-made looseleaf binder is too expensive, and partly because librarians, it seems, are implacably opposed to the looseleaf book as an object to be placed in their libraries. I regret this impracticality, for the idea is so beautifully simple and rational; and, besides, such a device would emphasize the fact that this is an edition not of a text, but of a document, the format of which should be determined by the ways in which it will be used.

Obviously the most exacting of my obligations to the reader would be the provision of cross-references. With this task in mind, I prepared two mechanical aids, which I will describe now although I was not to use them for some time. The first was a card file, which I shall call the reference file. I went through the standard American edition of the text and made dividers, first of all to mark off each episode and interlude in the text, with an inclusive page reference for each. I then subdivided each episode into smaller segments, briefly identifying each segment and noting its inclusive page reference. I ended up with a subdivision of the text into 100 segments, each sufficiently small and identifiable to allow me to find rapidly in the cards any passage in the text. The second aid was another card file, which simply divided 769 numbered cards (representing the total manuscript pages) into units of ten cards, so that I could rapidly locate the card for any page of transcription. I call this the footnote file. Each of these aids came into use at a certain stage of my procedures, which I shall now describe.

1 After visiting the Berg Collection of the New York Public Library in order to pick up the photoprints and verify them against the manuscript, I sat down beside a mountain of foolscap and transcribed, page for page, directly onto the typewriter, leaving blank spaces for any word which I could not decipher. This transcription I regarded as 'raw' - to be refined on subsequent journeys through the photoprints. I was content to leave it raw at this stage because the prime necessity was to plod steadily forward, and not to bog down. Virginia Woolf's hand is neither eccentric nor inherently difficult. She wrote in the common English script, using an old-fashioned straight pen, normally writing only on the right-hand page of her manuscript book, with the left-hand page reserved for notes and insertions. At the beginning of a day's work, it is a perfectly legible hand, and even elegant; when

she is writing at top speed - as, for example, in the concluding pages of the second draft - it is almost wholly illegible; and in between these extremes, an initial *r* frequently resembles an initial *s*, a terminal *n* will resemble a *g* or *y* or even a *z*, a lower case *e* will get laid on its back so that it resembles an *m*, and capitals will sometimes be indistinguishable from the lower case of the letter.

2 As I produced the raw transcription, I gave it to an assistant who proofread it closely against the prints, correcting errors of omission and commission, and pencilling in her reading of any illegibility which she believed she could decipher. The raw transcription and the first proofreading took almost exactly a year to complete.

3 I next went through the transcription, and made what I shall call a running record of the narrative. I wanted this on sheets of paper so that I could scan it rapidly. In this record I noted every appearance of any segment of the narrative which corresponded to the segments I had distinguished in my reference file, using for the purpose the brief descriptions I had already used in making up that file. But I made much more detailed identifications in the running record: I noted every change of speaker and identified briefly the content of his speech; described every segment that I knew I could not locate in the text; and noted every point at which every version of an interlude began. In the course of making this record, I corrected more errors and deciphered more illegibilities in the transcription.

4 I now returned again to page 1 of the transcription, armed with the reference file, the running record, and the text, in order to make up the cards which would be used for cross-references. A separate card is used for each footnote entry and on each card appears the number of the page of transcription for which it is a footnote, its particular footnote sign on that page, a brief identification of the passage being footnoted, and the revelant page number in the text. The running record enables me to locate the various versions of a passage in the transcription fairly easily; the dividers in the reference file help me to place the card in the slot for the

corresponding passage in the text; the transcription page number will permit me to shuffle cards when the notes are completed, so that I can collect all notes for a given page of transcription; and the brief description on each card will enable me to match all the notes pertaining to a specific passage. When this task is finished, I will have a file in which the references for all the manuscript versions of a specific passage will be gathered together, and placed in a sequence corresponding to the location of that passage in the text. There will also be a division of the file marked 'cannot locate'; and when I have completed the basic annotation, I will pull the pages of transcription to which these cards refer and will conduct a relentless search for corresponding passages in the text.

It is in preparing these footnotes that I confront a problem common to editors of any kind. How often should I annotate? How refined a set of cross-references are required? Theoretically, I could go on and on until I had located every place in which a given phrase occurs. There is of course no simple solution; but I have a short list of occasions on which I *must* annotate:

1 At the beginning of every version of an episode or interlude;
2 At the beginning of a passage which is located in a different position from its location in the text;
3 At the beginning of every version of a passage which does not appear in the text.

But such rules of thumb do not solve the problem, and must themselves be broken at times. For example, in the fourth episode of the text, at the farewell dinner, there occurs a passage of very brief speeches, a kind of antiphonal exchange. I provide cross-references for every version of the entire exchange, but do not footnote every change of speaker within it, even though the order of speakers varies from version to version in the manuscript and differs from their order in the text. I feel I have discharged my obligation to the reader if I direct him to all the pages on which this exchange begins: the rest he can discover for himself by reading. I want to help him work with this document, but I am not obligated to do all the work for him.

I will of course offer informative footnotes which refer only to the page on which they appear; such as a note to the effect that a passage is written in pencil, or that a verso entry appears opposite a certain point on the facing page, and so on.

5 When I conclude that I have gathered in my reference file all the notes I consider necessary, I will begin the process of making up the footnotes for each page of transcription. Let us suppose that I am annotating page 10. Observing the content of the first passage to be footnoted, I will turn to my reference file and pull all the cards for the various versions of that passage. Let us say there are three versions: the one on page 10, which I am annotating; another on page 68; and a third on page 411; all of them involving a reference to the final version on page 17 of the text. Turning to the footnote file, I will pull the cards for pages 10, 68, and 411. On each of them I write the page numbers of the others and the page number for the text. I return the reference cards for pages 68 and 411 to their location in the footnote file, keeping out the card for page 10, so that I can proceed to the next note. At the end of it all - as the last trump sounds - I will have in my footnote file a card for every page of transcription, with all the footnotes on it, arranged in their order of appearance on the page. From this card the typist will type in the notes as she prepares the final typescript from which the book will be produced.

6 My final effort to help the reader will involve the preparation of several supplementary aids.

a A Table of Contents, which will be constructed from the running record of the transcription and will identify and give the initial page number for those segments of the manuscript which correspond to the major divisions of the text into episodes and interludes. In order to use this table, the reader must be able to refer back and forth between it, the transcription, and the text; and therefore I will provide, immediately before the table, a brief description of the text, which will number every interlude and episode in the text, will provide inclusive page references for each in both editions, and will identify each episode by a brief title. Thereafter, in the table of contents itself, a passage will be identified simply as episode 2, or whatever, in order to keep the table as brief and concise as possible. At first, I inclined to give a more detailed breakdown of the contents; but this would involve reproducing the whole running record, which would be twenty or thirty pages long - too long to be useful. The table of contents, after all, is intended to serve as a supplement to the cross-references provided in the footnotes, not as a replacement for them; and its chief value will lie in its brevity. It will permit the reader to locate rapidly all the versions of a given episode, for purposes of comparison, and at the same time will throw into relief the distinctive structural features of each draft, a service which the footnotes do not perform and even prevent.

The episodes are easily identifiable by reference to the text; but the interludes remained in a state of flux for so long that it is doubtful whether I will be able, in most cases, to assign any one of them to any one interlude in the text. Rather than clutter the table of contents with a series of references for each interlude, I will simply note that an interlude begins on a given page, and save cross-reference for the footnotes.

b The second supplementary aid will be an index of speakers. In a book in which the narrative is delivered by six speakers, the development of a single speaker may well interest a student. Under the name of each speaker, therefore, I will first give a list of his aliases in the manuscript (the names changed a good deal in the early stages of composition), and will then list the page on which begins every speech assigned to him in the manuscript, or the text, or both.

c The final supplementary aid will be a collation of all the dates entered in the manuscript by Virginia Woolf with the dates of entries in *A Writer's Diary* which are relevant to *The Waves.*

If I may now direct your attention to the sample page

(shown in figure 1), let me first explain that this is a reproduction of my transcription, and is doctored for illustration. The final transcript, from which the edition will be produced by photo-offset, will make use of different sizes of type and types faces for the text of the transcription, the interlineations, the marginalia, and the footnotes.

1 *Pagination* The consecutive page number in the upper right corner of the sample is the number of this page and *only* this page in the whole manuscript. I found it necessary to establish this, my own, pagination for two reasons. First, Virginia Woolf did not paginate at all - why should she when she wrote in bound books of blank paper? Second, the pagination supplied by the cataloguers of the Berg Collection, however sound it may be from a bibliographical point of view, is extremely awkward from mine. They number *each* manuscript book consecutively, and they number *every* page, including the left-hand page, which is usually blank. Following their pagination would have forced me, and the reader, to identify each page by two numerals, the manuscript book number and the page number in that manuscript book. In addition, the reader would have to remember, or be told repeatedly, that any even-numbered page is in fact a verso page. Finally, it is clear that the manuscript books were simply so much blank paper to Virginia Woolf (the second draft, for example, begins immediately following the first draft, in the middle of the fourth manuscript book). For all these reasons, I made my own consecutive pagination for the entire manuscript; but I was obviously obliged to give the reader the pagination he will have to use when he goes to the Berg Collection to discover for himself how many mistakes I have made. This I do in the upper left corner.

2 *Footnotes* The passage at the top of the sample page prefaced by an asterisk occurs in episode 1 of the text, when the children are at their lessons. The roman I in the note precedes references to other versions in the first draft, which is also the first volume of my edition; roman II precedes the references to the second draft; and finally I give the page reference for the passage in the standard American edition (A 00) and the standard British edition (B 00).

1.9 5

*It was Jinny who had such difficulty with her lessons.

sitting

~~so that she sat~~ at the long table swaying her head from side to side;

while Louis, who was so ~~very~~ slow, ~~managed to write~~ yet

wrote what he did write so clearly that there could be no mistake.

Archie, the ~~subtle smiling~~ humourous boy, never very much

bothered about ~~the rest~~; he ~~did~~ had, for his age -- & they were

--

all about the same age, a remarkable address, surely, as though

~~when he was~~ [---] ~~long before this~~, in the cradle perhaps, his

seen oh yes. [mother]

he ~~had made the circuit, seeing~~ the rat or the flower, ~~having~~

~~considered them~~, no longer found anything ~~to~~ hateful ~~in them; or;~~

much amusing. It was hard to say. ~~Louis was John was~~

~~more~~ He was so well poised, that even then nobody,

~~however definite their own views~~, could unbalance him. Back he

†But

settled -- Susie, ~~was the consoler. Miriam was~~

~~taking~~ sobbed, ~~very bitterly, taking the broken~~ in great gulps &

[spasms,]

that day; ~~because hear~~ love had come, not to her, in the corner of the

garden. And there were many others; John, Philip, ~~Cass~~ Alice, Rachel

~~The fold of the napkin~~,

Figure 1 These two facing pages constitute one continuous manuscript page in *The Waves*; for ease of reproduction in this volume the page was split between paragraphs.

‡The moth quivered on the plaster wall; & the ~~thin~~ moon light ~~of very~~ coated jars & plants very thinly, & the ~~gr~~ plant leaning on its stick. ~~Meanwhile The~~ voice ~~of the sea~~ rolled over myriads of fresh pebbles & went out again. ~~The Almost nothing was clear. The room was very bare.~~

as if they were all white, almost colourless.

→And now the cock ~~broke the~~ crew. ~~It was all very~~ No sooner had one sound begun, than it was cut into; ~~the pale sun blank song of the birds~~ one bird sang; then stopped. Another started; then stopped. ←Yet in spite of its incoherence, the dawn of day was lovely; its azures, its saffrons, must be creeping [over the] sea. [-] ~~Fingers of light, must be pr~~ It was still too early for anything ~~solid~~ so solid as a bar of light; only on the horizon lay one clear line of paler blue, as if a ~~litt~~ shelf of glass rested here. The islands which in broad day ~~light~~ were as solid as the mainland, were now only phantoms. A ship could ~~have~~ sail~~ed~~ through them. Not enough light came ~~from the mor country,~~ even with all the windows uncurtained, to read by.

---

* I 3, 10, 68, 82; II 417; A 21, B 15
† I 13, 76; II 409; A 13, B 10
‡ I 2, 10, 41, 60, 69, 100; II 401, 404, 405, 406, 744; A 7, B 5
→← I 18, 46, 102, 124; II 452, 517, 523, 745; A 29, B 20

The passage footnoted with a dagger is the first version of Susan's reaction when she sees Jinny kiss Louis in the garden. I footnote this version on this page because, in the text, this passage *precedes* the incident of the children at their lessons. The second paragraph on the page, prefaced by a double dagger, is a version of the first interlude, which in the text, of course, precedes the whole of the first episode. By looking at the page references to the text in these notes, the reader can discern at once how the sequence of these passages on this page differs from their sequence in the text.

Although there are no examples on this sample page, there are passages, especially in the first draft, which have no parallel in the text. In the case of these, I provide cross-references within the manuscript and simply omit the final reference to the text.

3 *Illegibilities* Every illegibility is indicated by a blank space surrounded by brackets; and the only illegibility on the sample page, noted in the left margin, is also cancelled. Because Virginia Woolf's use of brackets was both infrequent and inconsistent (she often coupled a parenthesis mark and a bracket), I have reserved brackets as an exclusively editorial sign, and have regularized her practice by using parentheses. On rare occasions, I suspect it will be necessary to reproduce her brackets, but in such cases I will draw the brackets in ink to distinguish them from mine. One use of brackets as an editorial sign is illustrated along the right margin of the sample page. The words in brackets are words run over from the line to which they belong. In the final typescript from which the photo-offset will be made, many of these run-overs will disappear because the typist can control the distribution of type in the line. But those that remain will be placed immediately below the line to which they belong, in brackets.

4 *Cancellations* Because Virginia Woolf used a pen with an old-fashioned steel nib, cancellations have vexed me a good deal. The ink did not always flow, and one may discover a dim gouge in the page, followed by a stroke, followed by another gouge. I have searched hard for gouges; and I have

searched the context for help in determining what is cancelled and what is not. But when in doubt, I have transcribed only what my eye can see.

5 *Other marks* I have inserted on the sample page several diagonal cancellation marks and an insertion mark in order to illustrate one of the boons which photo-offset gives an editor of draft material. Such marks can be drawn in exactly as they are in the original. Photo-offset is not only much less expensive than set type, it is a much more flexible method for reproducing the original with clarity and precision.

So much for my attempt to explain some of my editorial principles, problems, and practices. I want to refer briefly now to the Introduction I must write for this edition. Aside from the usual information given in such introductions, I shall sketch some of the ways in which the manuscript may throw light on the text of *The Waves;* but in so doing, I shall be controlled, I hope, by my long-standing distaste for an editor who offers me a pristine text so that I can interpret it freely, and who then proceeds to tell me what it means. I shall attempt to articulate some of the questions which I believe the manuscript forces us to ask about the text, but shall not attempt to provide answers to them; I shall outline problems rather than solutions. In the process of doing this, I suspect I shall also be tempted to discuss certain problems and certain particular benefits which are generated by the study of draft material in general. Let me begin with an example. In the text of *The Waves,* and in the second draft, the last three episodes occur in this order: middle age, the reunion dinner at Hampton Court, Bernard's summing up. But in the first draft the sequence is: the reunion dinner, middle age, the summing up. Why was the sequence of two of these episodes reversed? The manuscript forces us to ask this question, but it provides no answer. In searching for an answer, a critic must hold in mind the effects produced by both these sequences; and this discipline may yield more than a specific answer to this specific question about *The Waves.* I believe that such a discipline, extended and enlarged by examining draft material for other texts, may lead the critic to fresh perceptions about the nature of *sequence* in narrative. The sustained effort to see texts in the context of their manuscripts involves a discipline of the critical imagination unlike the disciplines provided by the study of other contexts. That scarred and dropsical relation to the king has a unique *kind* of claim upon our minds. If enough people seriously engage in this kind of discipline, it may lead slowly to the realignment of fundamental critical presuppositions, to the formulation of new questions, to the rephrasing of old questions, to a sharper appraisal of our old instruments of analysis and to the invention of new instruments more delicate and precise.

All this is highly speculative; but I have been sustained by a growing conviction that the study of draft material can be an important, though as yet ill-defined, form of involvement not only with the specific text in question, but with the foundation and superstructure of criticism itself. It is an engagement which can proceed only through a much wider and closer scrutiny of many more such documents than has occurred thus far; and this scrutiny cannot occur unless more of these documents are edited and published. I could not have plodded on this far in my labours had I believed that this edition could do no more than illuminate a few aspects of one literary text; nor could I have gone on had I believed that it would become a solitary monument to the pedantic obsessions of its editor. I do not believe it will serve only its more obvious purposes; and I am confident that it will not remain a solitary sport.

A Note on Editing *The Interpreters* a Novel by Wole Soyinka

ELDRED D. JONES

The provision of critical editions of the works in English of the more significant of the African writers is an important task to be undertaken for the benefit of both African and non-African readers alike, but particularly for African readers. Because they often use the most sophisticated techniques of modern non-African literature, and write against the background of rich experience which involves, besides Africa, the whole ancient and modern world, African writers can leave their immediate potential readers, other Africans, far behind. Christopher Okigbo, the late Nigerian poet, is a good example of a writer who, until the recent spate of critical interest in his work, was considered incomprehensible by most African readers, even though much of his poetic apparatus derives from his traditional African background. He was by training a classical scholar and readily used his background of classical ideas to construct his own particular poetic world. The stylistic influence also of modern non-African writers, notably Eliot and Pound, on his writing has been frequently pointed out. Such a complexity might result in the works of writers being inaccessible to readers for whom English is a foreign language.

The advantage to non-African readers of having the works

of African writers presented against their African background is too obvious to need emphasizing. It so happens that Soyinka's novel, which is the subject of this article, owes its alleged difficulty, not to its African setting, but to its stylistic devices. It has few special difficulties for a non-African reader.

Wole Soyinka is a Nigerian writer, better known for his plays and poetry than for his prose. *The Interpreters*, in fact, is his only novel so far. The edition that is the subject of this article is a critical one providing an introduction and annotations.[1] The novel was first published by André Deutsch in 1965, and presents no textual problems. This text is the basis of the 1970 edition. The reason for the edition was a practical one - to make a significant work accessible to a larger readership. A widespread feeling, particularly in Africa, that the novel was 'difficult' discouraged many people from reading it. Convinced that it is one of the most important African novels written up to this time, I undertook this edition to ease the difficulties. These arose mainly from the technique of narration, and from the language which was often more suggestive than explicit but which was essential to the novel's effectiveness. A simplified version of *The Interpreters* would be a travesty.

Soyinka employs a technique of broken chronology, which involves frequent time shifts from the present to the past and back again, through the thought associations of the characters. These shifts in time would be strange to readers more used to sequential narration. Soyinka's use of the device can fortunately be illustrated with the help of passages at the beginning of the novel, and thus an initial stumbling block can be removed - many of the disappointed readers had lost their way in these opening pages and had given up. The hope is that similar shifts can be worked out by the

1 / The edition was published by Heinemann, London, in 1970, in their African Writers series. Its introduction and notes were published separately in *African Literature Today* 2 (January 1969).

reader himself who would be able to sense the transitions through clues in the text.

The first paragraph of the novel reads:

> 'Metal on concrete jars my drink lobes'. This was Sagoe, grumbling as he stuck fingers in his ears against the mad screech of iron tables. Then his neck was nearly snapped as Dehinwa leapt up and Sagoe's head dangled in the void where her lap had been. Bandele's arms never ceased to surprise. At half-span they embraced table and chairs, pushed them deep into the main wall as dancers dodged long chameleon tongues of the cloudburst and the wind leapt at them, visibly malevolent. In a moment only the band was left. (p. 7)

The opening sentence could be quite puzzling: ' "Metal on concrete jars my drink lobes." ' The juxtaposition of 'concrete' and 'jars' suggests a false grammatical association on a quick reading and this, along with the unfamiliarity of the coined physiological organs, 'drink lobes,' produces a strange shock. Soyinka's style is so far removed from cliché that he continually administers this kind of shock. (Soyinka sometimes invokes the cliché effectively as a silent comment on an action. An example is pointed out in a note to the passage on page 12 where Egbo makes a crucial choice by ordering the boatmen to ' "with the tide." ') The rest of this first paragraph assembles a number of details which by their economy and sometimes dramatic lack of sequacity present a scene of bustle and confusion in what becomes revealed as an open-air night club during a sudden rain storm. The author's approach is oblique but richly suggestive.

This brief paragraph was selected mainly for its early place in the work and not for any special difficulty; it illustrates Soyinka's method throughout the novel of supplying the pieces which when mentally put together produce the complete picture. The pieces are not always supplied at once; in the episode of Sagoe's encounter with Simi, for example, one piece is introduced on page 60 but the reader has to hold on to it until page 128 before it finally fits into place.

The 1970 edition points to details like these but hopes

not to ruin the effects by over-explaining them. The intention is not to relieve the reader of the expenditure of energy required by the muscular style of the novel. Rather it is to alert him to devices which might merely discourage by their seeming strangeness, and show how they contribute to the novel's effectiveness.

For example disjointed episodes in the novel are really connected by verbal and other associations. Again this technique is illustrated in the edition with a reference to a passage at the beginning of the novel. The night club scene discussed earlier is interrupted, seemingly without warning, on pages 7 and 8 by an episode on a creek. Once the company has gained shelter from the storm introduced in the first paragraph, Egbo becomes the centre of the narration.

> –Egbo watched the rising pool in which his polluted beer dissolved in froth. A last straggle of white clung stubbornly to the bamboo, rising with the water; the rest thinned fast under direct whipping off the roof.
> 'Well, I made a choice. I can't complain'
> Bandele looked up at him.
> 'Oh I was only having a chat with me and this talkative puddle.'
>
> Two paddles clove the still water of the creek, and the canoe trailed behind its silent groove, between gnarled tears of mangrove; it was dead air, and they came to a spot where an old rusted cannon showed above the water. It built a faded photo of the past with rotting canoe hulks along the bank, but the link was spurious. The paddlers slowed down and held the boat against the cannon. Egbo put his hand in the water and dropped his eyes down the brackish stillness, down the dark depths to its bed of mud. He looked reposed, wholly withdrawn.

In the passage beginning 'Two paddles,' as should soon become clear, Egbo is reliving a momentous water journey which involved a 'choice' glanced at in the remark - ' "Well, I made a choice ..." ' - whose suddenness startles Bandele - 'Bandele looked up at him.' Egbo had in fact just surfaced from his reverie, which the ensuing passage then goes on to describe. This sequence itself involves a distortion of the 'natural' order of events, since the reverie presumably took place before the remark ' "Well, I made a choice." ' Egbo's reverie in fact takes him further back in his life - into his childhood - than the momentous journey, before he returns to the real first scene of the novel, the night club. The reverie ends on page 17.

The aim of the edition was to demonstrate this fluid use of time as early as possible in the novel so that similar devices could be sensed by the reader as he proceeds. In spite of this assistance there are bound to be hasty leafings back on more than one occasion. Signposts are provided to the more important examples of this and similar devices later in the novel.

A look at only three opening paragraphs of *The Interpreters* may have suggested some of the characteristics of Soyinka's writing which could lead to difficulties - the 'drink lobes,' Soyinka's own contribution to human physiology is a convenient illustration - but he frequently performs feats of quick association which could puzzle the less responsive reader. Even a plodding reader, however, should finally get the metaphorical association of the waiter dressed in green with a fly, in the following passage.

Tray outstretched, Greenbottle advanced, circled him but Winsala seemed finally asleep.
'Enh? Abi 'e done sleep?' And Greenbottle tried to see the eyes beneath the cap. Winsala's patience was rewarded, an alert paw shot upwards and the tray flew up, caught Greenbottle on the proboscis and went clattering on the tile.

Greenbottle retracted wounded, underwent instant changes of ugliness. The buzz of his outraged comrades swelled the incident beyond proportion.

The unexpressed 'bluebottle' is the link, but 'circled,' 'proboscis,' 'buzz' explicitly reinforce the link. 'Paw' produces other metaphorical associations which further enrich the texture of the passage.

Not everything in the novel works out perfectly. One episode (on pp. 223-4), in which Noah, the disciple of Lazarus, seems to have failed a kind of ordeal by fire, shows obliqueness leading to obscurity. It is an editor's duty to point out his own failure to resolve such passages. Another unsatisfactory feature which I felt obliged to point to is the philosophy which Soyinka invents for Sagoe. Sagoe's rather esoteric attempt to explain fundamentals of life through the process of voiding the body's waste was going to be the subject of a thesis except that his professors rejected it - quite wisely, one feels. Up to this point the philosophy is a good joke; it also significantly highlights the impish irreverence which is part of Sagoe's character. But when one, even unconsciously, balances the amount of space devoted to it against any new significances produced, one experiences the uneasiness associated with a laboured joke.

The edition makes some attempt to put the novel in the context of Soyinka's other works. The reader who comes to *The Interpreters* after the plays and the poems would be prepared for the highly compressed language, as well as for the tricks with time. Even when they are not strictly relevant to a reading of the novel, parallels with Soyinka's other works suggest themselves, and some of these are pointed out. It is clear, for example, that the passages quoted below spring from the same imagination, an imagination fascinated by the sudden transformation from life to death which comes with a car crash. Sudden transformation is almost an obsessive theme in Soyinka's work. In the novel, one of the interpreters, Sekoni, dies in a car crash, and his death is thus described:

> A futile heap of metal, and Sekoni's body lay surprised across the open door, showers of laminated glass around him, his beard one fastness of blood and wet earth. (p. 155)

In Soyinka's poem 'Death in the Dawn' another victim of a car crash is similarly pictured as 'startled' ('surprised') at his instant translation:

> Brother
> Silenced in the startled hug of
> Your invention - is this mocked grimace
> This closed contortion - I?

The Road, a play which is preoccupied with death (particularly death on the road), naturally provides further examples:

> ... a madness where a motor-car throws itself against a tree - Gbram! And showers of crystal flying on broken souls.

Throughout this novel such fruitful associations with Soyinka's other work could be made. *The Interpreters,* sensitively read, constantly provides an illumination of ideas which appear in the poem and plays. Soyinka's highly condensed syntax, his fondness for metaphor, his allusiveness, his poetic style are all briefly illustrated in the introduction to the edition of the novel.

Unlike the plays and some of the poetry, *The Interpreters* does not depend to any great extent on a background of Yoruba ideas, even though it is firmly set in a Western Nigerian society whose traditional shrines jostle its university buildings. The pantheon of Yoruba gods functions here, but only in a limited way, as subjects for a painter's canvas. The characteristics attributed to them in Yoruba mythology are relevant to their portrayal on Kola's canvas, but that is all. (In *A Dance of the Forests*, by contrast, even the form of the play requires an understanding of the Yoruba mytho-theological background.) In any case Soyinka himself provided for the original edition of the novel a useful glossary of Yoruba words and expressions, as well as a list of the Yoruba deities mentioned, with their relevant attributes. The author here gives most of the primary material that would be strange to a non-Yoruba reader, who would be left to sense for himself the strange residues of the traditional presences in the atmosphere of the novel and in the actions of these young interpreters. The episode of Egbo's strange whim to pass the night under a railway bridge, naked and fearful in the presence of the god Ogun (p. 126), is, through its atmosphere of a communion with primary forces of nature, a reminder of the deep background of these modern Nigerians. One cannot help associating this rather mystical episode with Soyinka's own mystical communion with the same god Ogun, which produced his poem *Idanre,* published two years later than the novel.

The novel leads off through its characters into a wide background of experience - the arts, engineering, religion, travel, etc. - which might tempt an editor to over-gloss. I have tried to resist the temptation. Ikoyi (p. 111), a place name in Lagos, is glossed only to point out satirical suggestions which might be lost on a reader not familiar with the city. Baldwin's novel, *Giovanni's Room* (p. 47), is used by the homosexual Joe Golder as a bait; the nature of the work is briefly suggested in a gloss. References to the Mecca pilgrimage and the biblical stories - Esau and Jacob, and Jael and Sisera - seem to call for some help, and they are duly glossed. It is hoped that the edition's reticence does not leave many difficulties unattended to.

All that the editorial annotations can hope to provide is a key to a work which is very rich in texture and is in fact a mordant satire on the new society of contemporary Nigeria. The main satiric device is irony. There is a parade of corrupt judges, ignorant controllers of the mass media, complacent university professors who are made some of the individual butts of the satire, but eventually the satire is not against individuals but against a whole society which is hollow and rotten, which places a higher value on the façade than on the essence within. This idea is given physical reality in Soyinka's description of the offices of the *Independent Viewpoint,* a party newspaper, built in the heart of a slum, but having a perfumed executive toilet within. One of the most biting comments on the society as a whole is given in a passage describing a general chase of a petty thief; it conveys the suggestion of the basic injustice of a society which bears down hard on the small thief while lavishing adulation on the bigger thieves:

> Sagoe leapt off the bus and joined the throng - Run, Barabbas, run, all underdog sympathetic. Run, you little thief or the bigger thieves will pass a law against your existence as a menace to society. Sagoe followed them ... run, Barabbas from the same crowd which will reform

tomorrow and cheer the larger thief returning from his twentieth Economic Mission and pluck his train from the mud, dog-wise, in their teeth. (p. 114)

The satire is plain; indeed here the touch is heavier than is characteristic of Soyinka.

Editing *The Interpreters* was a labour of love rather than a scholarly exercise. It sprang out of a personal consciousness of the worth of a novel which is concerned with the very real problem of forging a life in modern West Africa where the old beliefs and sanctions are not cold. They lie smouldering beside the steel bridges, universities, and newspaper offices; patient when they are ignored, but ready to offer their clues to the total meaning of existence. Soyinka portrays the frustrations, the temptations, the corruptions, the beauties, and occasionally the rewards of a courageous search for meaning in all this confusion. The novel is, however, primarily a work of art. Its social relevance only makes it doubly valuable.

Members of the Conference

John D. Baird *Victoria College, University of Toronto*
A.M. Beattie *Carleton University*
G.E. Bentley, Jr *University College, University of Toronto*
Kenneth Blackwell *McMaster University; Mills Memorial Library, Bertrand Russell Archives*
William Blissett *University College, University of Toronto*
O M Brack, Jr *Center for Textual Studies, University of Iowa*
Matthew J. Bruccoli *University of South Carolina*
Gordon Coggins *Brock University*
Beatrice Corrigan *University of Toronto*
Jack P. Dalton *University of South Carolina*
Donald Eddy *Cornell University*
Richard Exner *University of California, Santa Barbara*
David Esplin *University of Toronto Library*
P.G. Gardner *Memorial University of Newfoundland*
John W. Graham *University of Western Ontario*
Francess G. Halpenny *Dictionary of Canadian Biography, University of Toronto Press*
Bruce Harkness *Kent State University*

James B. Harmer *Laurentian University*
Patricia Hernlund *Wayne State University*
Wm J. Howard New College *University of Toronto*
Jean C. Jamieson *University of Toronto Press*
Beverley Johnston *McGill-Queen's University Press*
D.A. Joyce *Trinity College, University of Toronto*
Richard G. Landon *University of Toronto Library*
Mr and Mrs Michael Millgate *University College, University of Toronto*
John McClelland *Victoria College, University of Toronto*
Mr and Mrs James B. Meriwether *University of South Carolina*
J.P. Morro CSB *Pontifical Institute, University of Toronto*
W.J.B. Owen *McMaster University*
Joseph Prescott *Wayne State University*
Thomas M. Paikeday *Holt, Rinehart and Winston of Canada*
S.P. Rosenbaum *Erindale College, University of Toronto*
John G. Slater *University of Toronto*
R.M. Schoeffel *University of Toronto Press*
John Stedmond *Queen's University*
R.J. Schoeck *St Michael's College, University of Toronto*
D.I.B. Smith *University College, University of Toronto*
Earle Toppings *Ontario Institute for Studies in Education*
Prudence Tracy *University of Toronto Press*
Peter West *Collier-Macmillan Canada Limited*
Jean Wilson *University of Toronto Press*